Irregular Enemies and the Essence of Strategy

Can the American Way of War Adapt?

Colin S. Gray

March 2006

FOREWORD

At present and probably for some years to come, America's enemies are of an irregular character. These irregular enemies necessarily wage war in modes that are largely unconventional.

In this monograph, Dr. Colin S. Gray considers irregular warfare in the light of the general theory of strategy and finds that that theory is fully adequate to explain the phenomenon. Rather less adequate, Dr. Gray suggests, is the traditional American way of war. The monograph offers a detailed comparison between the character of irregular warfare, insurgency in particular, and the principal enduring features of "the American way." It concludes that there is a serious mismatch between that "way" and the kind of behavior that is most effective in countering irregular foes.

Dr. Gray poses the question, Can the American way of war adapt to a strategic threat context dominated by irregular enemies? He suggests that the answer is "perhaps, but only with difficulty."

DOUGLAS C. LOVELACE, JR.
Director
Strategic Studies Institute

BIOGRAPHICAL SKETCH OF THE AUTHOR

COLIN S. GRAY is Professor of International Politics and Strategic Studies at the University of Reading, England. He worked at the International Institute for Strategic Studies (London) and at Hudson Institute (Croton-on-Hudson, NY) before founding a defense-oriented think tank in the Washington area, the National Institute for Public Policy. Dr. Gray served for 5 years in the Reagan administration on the President's General Advisory Committee on Arms Control and Disarmament. He has served as an adviser to both the U.S. and British governments (he has dual citizenship). His government work has included studies of nuclear strategy, arms control policy, maritime strategy, space strategy, and the use of special forces. Dr. Gray has written 19 books, most recently *The Sheriff: America's Defense of the New World Order* (University Press of Kentucky, 2004) and *Another Bloody Century: Future Warfare* (Weidenfeld and Nicolson, 2005; distributed by Casemate in the United States). In 2006 he will publish *Strategy and History: Essays on Theory and Practice* (Routledge). At present, he is working on a textbook, *War, Peace, and International Relations: An Introduction to Strategic History*, to be published by Routledge. Dr. Gray is a graduate of the Universities of Manchester and Oxford.

SUMMARY

Can the traditional American way of war adapt so as to be effective against irregular enemies? An endeavor to answer that question shapes and drives this inquiry. In order to address the question constructively, the author is obliged to explore and explain the nature and relations among three elements fundamental to our problem. Those elements are strategy, irregular enemies, and the American way of war. Carl von Clausewitz offered his theory of war in terms of a "remarkable trinity composed of primordial violence, hatred, and enmity . . . the play of chance and probability . . . and subordination, as an instrument of policy, which makes it subject to reason alone." He defined his task as a need "to develop a theory that maintains a balance between these three tendencies, like an object suspended between three magnets." The theoretical analogy may be imperfect, but still it is useful. Just as Clausewitz sought to explain war, and wars, as the product of inherently unstable relations among passion, chance, and reason, so this monograph has at its core the unstable interactions among irregular enemies, strategy, and the American way of war. Unlike Clausewitz, however, our purpose is not to develop or improve on general theory. Instead, the intention is to confront and try to answer the very specific question with which this summary began. To that end, strategic theory is deployed here pragmatically, as an aid to soldiers and officials who face challenges of a most pressing and serious character.

This inquiry defines and explains the essence of strategy. Next, it identifies what is distinctive about irregular enemies and the kinds of warfare they wage. Then the analysis proceeds to outline the fairly long-enduring traditional American way of war, and considers critically the fit between the many separate elements of that "way" and the requirements of sound practice in the conduct of warfare against irregulars. It concludes with a three-point argument which binds together the otherwise somewhat disparate topics and material.

The purpose of this monograph, beyond the commitment to offer some useful education, includes a desire to help explain better to the defense community both what it ought to know already, and — most especially — how the separate pieces of the trinitarian puzzle relate to each other. Much, probably most, of the content of the monograph is already familiar to many people, but it is not really familiar enough. Everyone interested in security affairs, surely, believes he/she understands strategy, irregular warfare, and the American way in war, but just how well are these elements comprehended, and are the consequences of their unstable interaction grasped securely? We think not. The monograph should make it difficult, not impossible, of course, for its readers to remain confused about the basics. These pages lay out in explicit detail the nature of strategy, irregular warfare, and — last, but not least — the long-preferred American way. But what does it all mean?

Both explicitly and implicitly, the monograph asks questions of the American defense community at all levels of behavior: strategic, operational, and tactical. The three conclusions explain the essential unity of the consequences of performance at these levels. We find that:

1. **War is war and strategy is strategy.** Strategically approached, there is only war and warfare. It does not matter whether a conflict is largely of a regular or an irregular character; Clausewitz's general theory of war and strategy applies equally to both. The threat or use of force is instrumental for political purposes. The kinds of warfare are of no relevance whatever to the authority of the general theory of strategy. In short, irregular warfare, waged by a range of irregular enemies, is governed by exactly the same lore as is regular warfare, viewed strategically.

2. **The United States has a persisting strategy deficit.** Americans are very competent at fighting, but they are much less successful in fighting in such a way that they secure the strategic and, hence, political, rewards they seek. The United States continues to have difficulty regarding war and politics as a unity, with war needing to be permeated by political considerations.

3. **American public, strategic, and military culture is not friendly to the means and methods necessary for the waging of warfare against irregular enemies.** The traditional American

way of war was developed to defeat regular enemies. It reflects many of the strengths of American society and culture. Alas, one military style does not suit all kinds of warfare equally well. The fit between the traditional "American way," and the requirements of counterinsurgency and counterterrorism, for example, falls far short of perfect. The pertinent question, therefore, is "Can that traditional way of war adapt so as to be effective against irregular enemies?" The answer of this monograph is "perhaps, but only with difficulty." The analysis and arguments presented here should help reduce the difficulty.

IRREGULAR ENEMIES AND THE ESSENCE OF STRATEGY: CAN THE AMERICAN WAY OF WAR ADAPT?

There are only wars.

Stuart Kinross, 2004[1]

Without some sense of historical continuity, Americans are likely to relearn the lessons of history each time they are faced with a low-intensity conflict. But what is more dangerous is the fact that during the relearning process Americans may suffer casualties and develop policy directions that can only lead to defeat.

Sam C. Sarkesian, 1984[2]

The conduct of small wars is in fact in certain respects an art by itself, diverging widely from what is adapted to the conditions of regular warfare, but not so widely that there are not in all its branches points which permit comparisons to be established.

Charles E. Callwell, 1906[3]

Introduction: The Return of Irregular Warfare.

Today the armed forces of the United States are struggling to contain and defeat an insurgency on the continent of Asia. Does that sound familiar? Strategic history is truly cyclical, a judgment resisted weakly and unsuccessfully by those who believe in progress in strategic affairs.[4] This monograph attempts what its title flags: to consider irregular warfare in the light of strategy, and—no less important—to examine the strengths and weaknesses of the historically dominant American way in warfare with reference to their consequences for the conduct of war against irregular enemies. The less challenging and controversial part of the monograph explains the relationship between irregular enemies and warfare on one hand, and the essence of strategy on the other. That essence is as certain and enduring a composite of ingredients as irregular enemies are disparate and, to a degree, unpredictable. By far the most difficult task undertaken here is the effort to answer the question in the

1

subtitle: "Can the American way of war adapt?" Is the United States, and not only its military tool, able to perform effectively, which is to say (grand) strategically, against irregular enemies? The principal mission of this inquiry is to probe systematically the elements of the American way of war in the light of what Americans have to be able to do, and the way they need to behave, in order to succeed in warfare against irregulars. Clausewitz is essential for our education, but as he insisted, though his general theory can help prepare us for the specific challenges we actually face, it can never "construct an algebraic formula for use on the battlefield."[5]

After a decade wandering in the policy and strategy wilderness, we strategists, in common with our politicians, have returned to a security context marked by a clear definition of era-defining threat. Strategists thrive on bad news. When it does not really exist, we do our best to invent it. Any strategic theorist worthy of the title can put together a menacing-looking threat briefing at the hint of a contract. The difficulty was that for a decade, from 1991 to 2001, few people believed our professional pessimism. In January 1994 I gave my inaugural lecture at the University of Hull in which I described the 1990s as an interwar period.[6] Some people found this to be shockingly atavistic. Surely, peace had broken out and, despite the host of more or less irregular wars underway at the time, large-scale war between states was now obsolete, or at least obsolescent. To talk of the 1990s as an interwar period seemed to some to be almost criminally backward-looking.

Well, here we are in 2006, and the Department of Defense (DoD) has issued a document with the imposing title, *National Defense Strategy of the United States of America*. The first sentence on page one of this august offering states without qualification, "America is a nation at war."[7] I hesitate to say, "I told you so," but I will say it anyway. Bad times *always* return in world politics. I do not know how many Americans feel as if they are at war, since not too many of war's characteristic hardships are being suffered by most people. I can assure you, though, that America's allies in Europe certainly do *not* feel themselves to be countries at war. One of the burdens of greatness is that the sheriff of world order is obliged to undertake, quite disproportionately, the heavy lifting for security on behalf of what we term, not without some irony, the international community.[8]

The no-name post-Cold War era is well and truly over: it detonated on September 11, 2001 (9/11). For a decade, the threat board had been misleadingly naked of major strategic menace. Without the True North of the Soviet threat by which to set a reliable guiding vector, the American defense community did not really know what it was about or, more important, why it might be about it. For the better part of 10 years, we debated the idea and meaning of a Revolution in Military Affairs (RMA). This exciting concept appealed to historians and to the many technophiles among us. But the debate was not exactly overburdened with strategic argument. Historically viewed, strategic thought, as a practical subject, tends to slumber between episodes of security alarm. The French philosopher Raymond Aron made this point exactly, when he wrote in 1968 that "Strategic thought draws its inspiration each century, or rather at each moment of history, from the problems which events themselves pose."[9] This is the reason why bookshop shelves today are groaning under the burden of good, bad, and ugly works on terrorism and insurgency. Only 5 or 6 years ago, it was a struggle to find anything on irregular unpleasantness. Those of us with gray hair will recall that Nikita Khrushchev's general declaration of support for wars of national liberation, and the enthusiastic response of the Kennedy administration to that challenge, sparked a similar flurry of studies of guerrilla warfare and related topics. No doubt some 30 or 40 years from now, in best or worst cyclical fashion, a new wave of irregular strategic happenings will trigger yet another burst of writing on "small wars" (wars between regulars and irregulars).[10] Another generation of strategic thinkers will rediscover the obvious, or at least they will rediscover what we know today. They will invent an impressive-sounding concept, some equivalent to Fourth Generation Warfare, and give dazzling briefings to credulous officials in need of an icon of strategic assuredness.[11]

The idea that strategy has an essence is deeply attractive. It sounds like something incredibly rare and valuable which could be bottled and sold. Perhaps, belatedly, I can make my fortune selling Gray's "essence of strategy." Unfortunately, American understanding of strategy, and sound practice of it, is almost desperately rare.

Strategic thinking and behavior worthy of the name are endangered activities in this country. This is hardly a stunningly original insight. But familiar though the criticism should be, it loses none of its bite for its longevity. Much as the U.S. defense community periodically is prodded by irregularist anxiety to worry about insurgency and terrorism, so from time to time it remembers the value of strategy. Many American defense professionals do not really know what strategy is or how it works.[12] After all, responsibility for it is well above their pay grades, but they know that it is a Very Big and Very Important Matter. The pattern has been one wherein a politician or two, or a senior official, with a personal interest, has lit the fire of genuinely strategic discussion. The fire flares brightly for a brief spell, but then dies away for want of fuel. The fire is not fed because there is not much demand for the heat and light of truly strategic argument in the United States. Ours is not quite a strategy-free environment, but such a characterization errs less than we would like to admit.

Now that I have somewhat prepared the battlespace, it is high time to declare the plot of this inquiry.

The Plot, with Caveats.

I shall make an argument with three intimately connected points. In addition to the three points that carry the main burden of the argument, I offer six important caveats that bear particularly upon the contemporary debate over how to respond to irregular enemies. These are controversial.

1. **War is war and strategy is strategy.** Forget qualifying adjectives: irregular war; guerrilla war; nuclear war; naval strategy; counterinsurgent strategy. The many modes of warfare and tools of strategy are of no significance for the nature of war and strategy. A general theory of war and strategy, such as that offered by Clausewitz and in different ways also by Sun-tzu and Thucydides, is a theory with universal applicability.[13] Because war and strategy are imperially authoritative concepts that accommodate all relevant modalities, a single general theory of war and strategy explains both regular and irregular warfare. Irregular warfare is, of course, different from regular

4

warfare, but it is not different strategically. If one can think strategically, one has the basic intellectual equipment needed in order to perform competently in either regular or irregular conflict.[14] Needless to add, understanding and performance are not synonymous.

2. **The United States has shown a persisting strategy deficit,** which reflects and feeds a political deficit in its way of war.[15] If you do not really function strategically, it does not much matter how competent you are at regular, or irregular, warfare — you are not going to collect the political rewards that American blood and money have paid for. American military power has been as awesome tactically as it has rarely been impressive operationally or strategically. Fighting should be guided by a theory of victory, otherwise the result tends to be "a strategy of tactics," as Andrew Krepinevich observed of the United States in Vietnam.[16] It is worth noting that the German armed forces in both world wars suffered from the same malady. Clausewitz did his best to educate his readers such that they could not be confused about the night-and-day difference between strategy and tactics, but, alas, his wisdom has not always dropped onto fertile soil. One would think that the following indelible definition and explanation must defy even determined efforts at misunderstanding. Probably it is the fate of Clausewitz more often to be ignored than misinterpreted. He advised that,

> Strategy is the use of the engagement for the purpose of the war. The strategist must therefore define an aim for the entire operational side of the war that will be in accordance with its purpose. In other words, he will draft the plan of the war, and the aim will determine the series of actions intended to achieve it: he will, in fact, shape the individual campaigns and, within these, decide on the individual engagements.[17]

3. **American public, strategic, and military culture is not friendly to the waging of irregular warfare,** which is to say, not friendly to the conduct of the only kind of warfare that can be effective against irregular enemies. There is a traditional American way of war, outlined below, and its features do not

favor the strengths required to succeed against irregulars.[18] In the 1960s and more recently, American military culture has proved resistant to making radical adjustments in its style of warfare in order to meet the distinctive challenges posed by an irregular enemy. In both periods, new technology was harnessed to "the American way" in the expectation, or hope, that the confining rules for effectiveness in irregular combat could be broken. Sun-tzu's insistence upon the need for self-knowledge in war is so familiar as to be a cliché.[19] But it is so essential to the plot of my story that I shall not be deterred from emphasizing his argument. *There is no little danger that the American military transformation now underway may disappoint in the benefits it confers.* The principal problems will be neither cunning asymmetrical enemies, nor even a shortage of funds to carry it along. Instead, the prospective gains from America's military transformation will be limited, if not frustrated, by the working of American public, strategic, and military culture. If one does not really "do strategy," it will not much matter whether one's armed forces are transformed or not. The issue is not only, or not primarily, How good will U.S. forces be tactically and operationally? Rather is it, How will they be used? And to achieve what ends will they be committed? Will those ends be selected and exploited by a coherent theory of victory so as to promote a desirable postwar political context?

In sum, the U.S. armed forces face two very different challenges to their effectiveness. First, their efforts are ever liable to be poorly rewarded because the United States has a persisting difficulty using force in strategically purposeful ways. Second, whether or not the country can raise its game and function strategically, American forces have had a long preferred style in warfare that is not well-suited to conflict with irregular enemies. These remain major challenges today.

The three elements that constitute the argument of this analysis do not make agreeable reading for those who are concerned to improve America's effectiveness as the main guardian of the current world order. I lay stress on the potency of culture because it is a concept that is easily misused. Today it is popular, at long last I must add, to point to the need for greater cultural awareness of enemies and allies. Some 30 years ago, or even 20, it was not.[20] Major General Robert Scales has called for a new culture-centric American approach to warfare.[21] He is largely correct. But *the* problem, the real problem, is with us and our culture, and that problem truly is more of a *condition* than a challenge to be overcome. We may transform the U.S. armed forces in some respects, but it may not be possible to transform a preferred way of war that expresses enduring cultural realities. To risk banality, America is what it is, and its strategic culture faithfully reflects American historical, social, ideological, and material realities.[22]

Strategic history is hugely complex. This complexity is a happy hunting ground for professional historians, who thrive on the rich uniqueness and contingency of events. But for strategic theorists, defense analysts, and policy advocates and policymakers, complexity usually is anathema. After all, strategy is a practical business and the holy grail is not perfect knowledge or elegant theory, but rather solutions to real-world problems that work well enough. The U.S. defense community is more than amply populated with theorist-advocates who offer patent strategic medicines of variable promise as the answer to current woes. What the medicines have in common is that they tend to contain a single Big Idea, and, as powerful theories are wont to do, they simplify that complexity of which we have just spoken. Generally speaking, the Big Idea has merit, sometimes even great merit. Nonetheless each Big Idea, each patent solution to America's contemporary strategic dilemmas, needs to be accompanied by a health warning. What follows are seven caveats to the triadic argument presented above. They do not invalidate or contradict that argument, but they combine to shout *caveat emptor!* These reservations have a direct bearing on judgment as to whether the American way of war is likely to prove sufficiently adaptable to be effective in combating irregular enemies.

The first caveat warns of the danger of imposing an undue clarity of strategic distinction between regular and irregular warfare. It is a highly expedient distinction, and it is one which is easily defensible. Moreover, it is an important difference. As with all of these caveats, the fault lies not with the idea, but rather with its exploitation in an oversimplified manner. Bear in mind the ambiguity about the notion of "irregular enemies." That can mean enemies of any genus who choose to fight in an irregular mode; or it may refer to foes who are deemed to be irregular by definition because they are not the licensed sword arms of officially recognized polities. In practice, many wars have been waged both regularly and irregularly, sometimes simultaneously, and often with shifting emphases. Vietnam, 1965-75, was a classic example of a war characterized by all modes of combat. Prior to Tet 1968, the war was primarily unconventional and irregular on the part of the Viet Cong, but there was that complicating, growing presence of People's Army of Vietnam units. After Tet, for reason of the debilitating attrition suffered by the irregulars and the failure of a general rising to occur, the war became ever more regular. Iraq in 2004-05 has witnessed irregular violence aplenty, but occasionally that violence has been manifested as highly organized insurgent action in defense of symbolic or important urban terrain. The beginning of wisdom probably is to be achieved by reacquainting oneself with Mao Tse-tung's three-stage theory of protracted revolutionary war.[23] Political agitation, guerrilla warfare, and regular conventional combat may be distinct phases in a struggle, but they can be undertaken in parallel, and, if one has overreached, he can step back from a phase.

This caveat against undue neatness in the categorization of conflict carries the warning that one size of military response probably will not fit the whole of the conflict in question, let alone the whole of the military context of an apparently emerging era.

The second caveat is the rather brutal point that merely to understand how insurgency works, and therefore how counter-insurgency (COIN) should be pursued, is not necessarily to be able to succeed at COIN. To those whose military education has been overwhelmingly regular and conventional, the secrets of COIN may appear exotic, not to say counterintuitive. Indeed, as we shall explain later, the requirements of COIN do pose what amounts to a full frontal challenge to the dominant traditional American way of war. But the international experience of COIN, successful and otherwise, has yielded a tactical and operational lore that is beyond intelligent challenge. To state the matter directly, we know how to do COIN. There is no mystery to it. It is not a dark art capable of mastery only by a relatively few elite soldiers with colored berets. Nonetheless, in conflict after conflict, the most elementary, yet vitally important, rules for behavior in COIN have a way of being flouted. The results are typically, predictably, unfortunate.

I would like to be able to claim that the requirements of COIN are so well understood that the problem, self-evidently, must lie with the impediments to implementation. However, that may be too generous a view. It is at least plausible to argue that some missionary work remains to be done before insurgency and COIN are comprehended as well as their regular counterparts.[24] Of course, ignorance is some form of excuse. It would be more difficult to excuse incompetence at COIN if the military and its political masters do understand the distinctive challenge, but elect to behave in the manner that they prefer, regardless. This monograph is concerned not so much about the state of understanding of COIN in the U.S. armed forces, but rather about the difficulties that impede their ability to translate that comprehension into effective performance. To understand is not necessarily to be able to behave appropriately.[25]

Caveat three is a reminder of what we should know already, but can be apt to forget when we try to turn conviction into capability and behavior. And by behavior I refer to action at all levels from tactical up to the grand strategic and even to high policy. Specifically, irregular enemies and irregular forms of warfare do not, and can never, present us with a single challenge that calls for a single master doctrinal response. Recent analyses by Steven Metz and Raymond Millen, as well as by Michael Morris — all in work sponsored by the Strategic Studies Institute of the U.S. Army War College, one must add — point out that insurgencies can be of a liberation or a national variety, and even that binary distinction lends itself to much further fine-tuning.[26] Morris's fascinating prize essay on al Qaeda speaks all too eloquently and persuasively to the variety of contexts for irregular conflict, the complexity of the connections between terrorism and insurgency, the ability of organizations to shape-shift quite radically, and the wide range of tactics that irregulars can employ in different circumstances. In Iraq, to select an example not totally at random, the motive force of ethno-religious opportunism in a context of some political chaos, has led insurgent terrorists to neglect the hearts and minds of rival communities in favor of brutal military atrocities. That kind of irregular enemy has to be defeated, yes defeated, in a manner which even Ralph Peters would unreservedly approve.[27] So the clear message in this caveat, which we develop later, is that the U.S. Army must transform itself to be more adaptable. It cannot apply a simple template or rely on power-point wisdom that promises victory over irregulars in "five easy steps." Each historical case is different. It is only at the level of strategy that one size fits all.

Caveat four is that the theory and practice of COIN should not be regarded as a panacea. COIN doctrine and capabilities may become fashionable in desperate reaction against the slim rewards from an aggressively pursued attritional strategy. When a mode of warfare is blessed officially and attracts widespread favorable notice, the critical faculties of new devotees often take a vacation. Classic COIN methods will not always be feasible, no matter how expert are the military practitioners and their civilian partners. COIN takes time, usually a great deal of it. Also, it requires a highly plausible political story and framework to support and advance. The necessary political underpinning for COIN may or may not be available. Moreover, the historical slate may not be sufficiently clean. The would-be COINers might well have prejudiced their mission fatally through the manner of their previous conduct of warfare, which is to say conduct prior to their serious resort to the COIN option. In short, COIN expertise and capabilities are essential and frequently will bear fruit. But they need some permissive conditions, not the least of which is the political tolerance of the American public with respect to an enemy who is using the war's temporal dimension as a weapon.[28] There is some danger that the American defense community today, having rediscovered the obvious merits of COIN, will respond with a cry of "Eureka," and proceed as if there is something magically effective about it as the all-purpose solution to many irregular enemies. To repeat, COIN strategy is not a panacea.

Caveat number five, still on the COIN theme, is the intentionally rather subversive thought that it may not be politically sensible, or strategically profitable, for American forces to be extensively engaged in counterinsurgency operations. This caveat bears on my final warning note, treated below as caveat seven, on the problems with culture. There is no question but that the U.S. armed forces,

and the Army most especially, need to be adept at COIN. Similarly, there is no doubt that COIN, in common with the Special Forces, was not exactly held in high official regard for many years.[29] There was, indeed there is, a capability and doctrinal deficit to make up. However, recognition that COIN prowess is at a premium in the global strategic context of today does not mean that it should be practiced very often by Americans. Simply because America's traditional way of war, favoring firepower, mobility, and an aggressive hunt for the main body of the foe, is apt to be ineffective against elusive irregular foes, it does not necessarily follow that COIN, by Americans, is the superior alternative. As a general rule, the heavy lifting in COIN should be performed by local forces, regular and irregular, military and civil. It would be inappropriate for the U.S. superpower to commit a large fraction of its armed forces, its Army in particular, to COIN duties. That activity can be performed successfully only by those who truly have the benefit of local knowledge and who intend not merely "to stay the course," but literally to stay. Americans can help (as well as sometimes hinder). But history and common sense both tell us that, inevitably, the more active American soldiers are in providing security for local clients, the more they undermine the political legitimacy of those clients.

My sixth caveat reminds that war and warfare are different concepts, and the difference is a matter of great importance. War is a total relationship—political, legal, social, and military. Warfare is the conduct of war, generally by military means. A narrow focus upon warfare proper, which is natural enough for armed forces, can obscure the need to function grand strategically, in doing which military behavior is only one dimension of the effort, albeit a vital one. In war with irregular enemies, actual warfare is unlikely to be the dominant mode of fruitful engagement. Since irregular foes will rarely concentrate and present themselves for open battle, the COIN struggle must largely take the form of political, intelligence, economic, social, and police activity, always supported by the heavy mailed first when opportunity beckons. Busy professionals with orders to follow typically are not oversensitive to context. But in wars of all kinds, warfare, bluntly stated, fighting, occurs in the context of the whole war, and it needs to be conducted in such a way that it fits the character of the war and thereby yields useful strategic effectiveness.

When the key distinction and relationship between war and warfare are not understood, the inevitable result is misdirected warfare, virtually no matter whether it is prosecuted efficiently.[30] We will let Clausewitz restate this caveat. He insists that "Everything in strategy is very simple, but that does not mean that everything is very easy. Once it has been determined, from the political conditions, what a war is meant to achieve and what it can achieve, it is easy to chart the course."[31] This final judgment is a Clausewitzian exaggeration, but he lays proper emphasis upon the nesting of military action, and the direction of that action by strategy, within the political context of the whole war.

My seventh and final caveat to the grand argument of this monograph is a warning parallel to that already issued concerning COIN theory and technique. Specifically, the undoubted significance of culture—public, strategic and military—in war, warfare, and strategy, recognized today as never before in recent times at least, is encouraging its elevation to the status of panacea. Appreciating the disadvantages of their local ignorance. American soldiers wisely endorse cultural awareness, if not expertise, as a key, perhaps the key, to the achievement of enhanced effectiveness. Obviously for COIN to be successful, cultural education is not merely desirable, it is literally essential. This monograph is not at all critical of the armed forces' new-found enthusiasm for education in war's cultural dimension. On the contrary, this author has campaigned for a quarter-century on behalf of just such a development.[32] The problem lies with the iconic adoption of culture as *the* answer. It is not. Recognition of the importance of culture is a part of the answer to the question of how to be effective in war against irregular (and regular!) enemies. But culture is a difficult concept to define and grasp. Even if grasped, it is extremely difficult to deal with or function in an alien culture of marked variance from one's own. Moreover, culture does not encompass all that matters in the waging of war. For example, no measure of cultural empathy would suffice to compensate for a missing political framework or for military incompetence.

The United States has two distinct problems in coping with the subject of this inquiry, problems that are flagged with scant subtlety in the title. Problem one is what I will call a "strategy deficit." The United States often has difficulty with strategy because, unsurprisingly, the

"normal" theory of American civil-military relations does its best to close down the strategy bridge that should unite politicians and soldiers in an unequal but never-ending dialogue over means and ends.[33]

The second problem is the challenge of coping with irregular enemies. As we discuss below, there is difficulty in adapting what fairly may be termed the traditional American way of war in a manner such that it can be effective against unlike, or asymmetrical, enemies.

It is perhaps arguable which of the two problems is the more serious, the strategy deficit or the cultural hindrances to adaptation to meet irregular foes. It might be argued that a new excellence in COIN, resting in part on a military performance enhanced by education in cultural awareness, will solve most of America's current dilemmas in dealing with irregular enemies. I decline to believe this new excellence would work, valuable though such a development would be. It is the firm opinion of this author that, unless America "does strategy," which is to say relates military and other means to its political ends in a purposeful, realistic, and adaptable way, improvements in military prowess ultimately must yield disappointing results.

The Essence of Strategy.

The key to strategy, certainly to thinking strategically, is the simple and rather off-putting question, "So what?" Strategists are not interested in the actual conduct of regular or irregular war. Their concern is what that conduct means for the course and consequences of a conflict. Tactical and operational excellence is always desirable, even if not always strictly necessary. Since, inter alia, warfare is a competition in learning between imperfect military machines, fortunately one need only be good enough. Tactical excellence is quality wasted if it is not employed purposefully to advance political goals. Of course, this is much easier to advocate than to do. Recall the old saying that "nothing is impossible to the person who does not have to do it." So what is strategy and how should one characterize its invaluable essence? What should be poured into those bottles of "Essence of Strategy?" I will suggest four overlapping ingredients as together constituting my preferred "essence."

First, following Carl von Clausewitz (who else), I must insist that strategy is about the use made of force and the threat of force for the goals of policy.[34] It ought to be hard to confuse the crucial distinction between behavior and its consequences. Nonetheless, many people manage to do so with consummate ease. "Strategic" does *not* mean very important, nuclear, independently decisive, or long-range. No weapon or mode of warfare, including terrorism, can be inherently strategic. All can have strategic effect. I freely admit that the vital concept of strategic effect is as hard to assess as it is central to proper understanding of our subject.

Second, strategy is all about the relationship between means and ends. Again, this is easy to specify, but fiendishly difficult to manage competently. It is always tempting to adopt the attitude that we warriors will win the fights and let politics take care of itself. Or, for a cognate approach, if we keep winning tactically, our strategy will flow agreeably from the cumulative verdicts of the battlefield. In practice, a war may thus be waged all but innocent of political guidance beyond an injunction to win. If the politicians focus on ends, as they should, and soldiers are consumed with means, it is probable that no one will be keeping open the strategy bridge that should be linking military means with political goals. There needs to be a continuous, albeit "unequal," dialogue between civilian and soldier. War and warfare are permeated with political meaning and consequences. A competent supreme command knows this and behaves accordingly. This dialogue, however, carries implications for civilian participation in military decisions in wartime which run contrary to the preferred military way in American civil-military relations.[35]

Third, if the strict instrumentality of force is not to be neglected or forgotten, and this is *the* most important ingredient in the essence of strategy, there has to be a constant dialogue between policymaker and soldier. Policy is nonsense if the troops cannot do it "in the field." Or, looking at it from another angle, the troops may be so effective in action that policy is left gasping far behind the unexpected opportunities opened by events. *On War* tells us that "[t]he conduct of war, in its great outlines, is therefore policy itself." The reader has already been told that "at the highest level, the art of war turns into

14

policy—but a policy conducted by fighting battles rather than by sending diplomatic notes."[36]

Fourth and finally, in case the point should fade from view under the pressure of military events, politics must rule. To quote another Clausewitzian maxim, "War is simply a continuation of political intercourse, with the addition of other means."[37]

The most essential of the four ingredients that, when mixed, become the essence of strategy, is the *instrumentality* of the threat or use of force. In practice, the pressures and demands of the actual waging of war have a way of relegating policy purpose to the background. All too often, policy may seem to serve war, rather than war serve policy.

One may well ask, if the essence of strategy is so simple, why is it so difficult to "do strategy" well? I will suggest a few answers. First, strategy by its essential nature is extraordinarily difficult to do.[38] Strategy is the bridge connecting the military instrument with the guidance of political purpose. Strategic expertise is neither military skill nor is it policy wisdom. It is the use of the military for political ends. Who is expert in strategy? Neither soldiers nor politicians are trained strategists. Indeed, excellence as a soldier on one side, and high political gifts on the other, are both off the mark as proof of strategic competence. Moreover, it is not entirely self-evident that competence in strategy can be taught. After all, by definition it requires the exercise of judgment about the value of one currency, military effort, in terms of another, political effect. Since war, at its core, is a contest of wills, the judgment required of the strategist strictly requires knowledge and skills that are unlikely to be widely available, if they are available at all. Not for nothing did Clausewitz claim that "[w]ar is the realm of chance."[39]

The second difficulty worth highlighting is the cultural and skill-bias contrast between the soldier and the civilian politician. This problem area is especially relevant to the American context and its dominant traditional way of war. Theory insists that policy and military means must march together, indeed they are one and the same, though with policy in the driving seat. However, policy goals, war and peace aims, should be chosen, and perhaps periodically revised, only in the light of military probabilities. All too obviously, the professional soldier and the no less professional politician, though culturally both American, in fact inhabit quite distinctive subcultural universes that have different rules and are marked by distinctive skill biases. In practice, true two-way communication of often unwelcome news can be difficult. Clausewitz does not address this problem, beyond offering the sage advice that "a certain grasp of military affairs is vital for those in charge of general policy."[40] Well, it may be vital, but what if it is missing? Or what if the politicians and generals do not respect, like, or trust each other? What if they do not share certain key values? To put the matter directly, how much influence should America's Commander-in-Chief be willing to exert over the direction and course of military events in time of war?[41] Should the President leave military decisions to the military, even though he or she knows from Clausewitz, and from historical experience, that warfare is inalienably political in its consequences?

Third, although the concept of strategic effect is crystal clear as an abstraction, how, exactly, is it to be measured? Just what is the exchange rate between military success and desired political consequence? Especially in the conduct of warfare against irregulars, what is the legal currency for the measurement of strategic effect? It is easily understandable, albeit unfortunate, why the mystery of strategic effect is apt to be solved by soldiers and officials who seize upon whatever can be counted as they take the default choice of favoring attrition. Bodies, pacified villages, reopened roads, declining incident rate, pick your preferences. Again, one must cite *the* strategist's question, "So what?" The strategist must know what military behavior means for the political purpose of the enterprise. Body counts need to be interpreted for their strategic value. They cannot simply be declared triumphantly as tactical achievements with self-evident meaning.

Fourth, strategy is difficult to do as an orderly and well-integrated exercise in the matching of means to ends because of the high inconvenience of the semi-independent behavior of an intelligent enemy. Under the exigencies of actual war against a live and somewhat unpredictable enemy, regular or irregular — it does not matter which — military necessity may compel military behavior that is very undesirable in its political consequences. Remember the grim irony from Vietnam: "We had to destroy the village in order to save it."[42] It is amazing how often supposed defense experts and strategic thinkers neglect to take proper account of the enemy on his own terms.

Finally, friction and the other elements of the climate of war, which is to say, "danger, exertion, uncertainty, and chance," are entirely capable of thwarting the best laid of strategic plans.[43] Also, bad weather, human error, and other inconveniences are not to be discounted. Things always go wrong. That is to be expected. A sound strategy is one that is tolerant of some of history's unpleasant surprises. Adaptability must be regarded as a cardinal military virtue.

Irregular Warfare.

Strategy is strategy regardless of circumstance, but the military and related behavior that strategy guides and exploits differ radically from case to case. As usual, our Prussian philosopher was as clear as could be on this vital matter.

> [T]his way of looking at it [war as an instrument of policy] will show us how wars must vary with the nature of their motives and of the situations which give rise to them. The first, the supreme, the most far-reaching act of judgment that the statesman and commander have to make is to establish by that test [political motives behind policy] the kind of war on which they are embarking, neither mistaking it for, nor trying to turn it into, something that is alien to its nature. This is the first of all strategic questions and the most comprehensive.[44]

The U.S. armed forces excel at high- and mid-intensity regular warfare. As explained earlier, regular and irregular modes of warfare often coexist. Also, it is true that elite units of regular forces are trained to wage war irregularly or unconventionally.[45] For the other side of the coin, irregular soldiers do not always confine their combat to a guerrilla style. They will stand and fight in a regular manner either when they have no choice, or, more likely, when they believe they have a crushing tactical advantage over some isolated element of the regular enemy's forces. We should recall that following the destruction of most of the fighting power of the Vietcong in the Tet Offensive and the clashes that came in its wake, the Vietnam war

17

became ever more regular in style. Paradoxically, with the change in command at Military Assistance Command-Vietnam (MACV) from General William Westmoreland to General Creighton Abrams (formerly a George Patton protégé of armored maneuver) in March 1968, the American effort spearheaded by the intelligent and already existing Civil Operations and Revolutionary Development Support program, reaped real dividends from its proper conduct of COIN.[46] Meanwhile, the enemy was condemned to expose himself to repeated regular defeat. None of which really mattered, of course, because the American political center of gravity of the war was well on the path to self-destruction.

It is plain to see that irregular enemies and irregular warfare comprise richly varied ranges of possibilities. But since this monograph has no ambition to be encyclopedic in its coverage, the focus here is on one slice of the irregularity spectrum, albeit by far the most important. Specifically, the purpose of this discussion is to provide a clear marker, a standard, against which, in the next section, we can appraise the traditional American way of war.[47] If America's future strategic history is going to be heavily populated with irregular enemies, foes who certainly will be obliged to fight irregularly save in truly exceptional circumstances, it is necessary for us to have a clear understanding of the distinctive character of the irregular strategic challenge. I must emphasize, yet again, that it is only the character of the strategic challenge that is distinctive, not its nature.

As the Army proceeds with its long-haul transformation, it must never forget that in the future it may well (indeed, in the opinion of this theorist, it will) have to face competent regular enemies as well as a crowd of irregular foes. However, there is relatively little likelihood of the Army finding itself improperly prepared with ideas, doctrine, trained people, organization, and equipment for regular warfare, although it could happen. Nonetheless, this analysis is dealing with trouble enough in the high realms of strategy and, at this juncture and later, of irregular warfare. We elect not to venture here into the woods of controversy over the future of regular, conventional combat.[48] Instead, our focus is on insurgency and terrorism. The irregular enemies alluded to in the title of this monograph are assumed to be insurgents and terrorists. The two categories overlap, although in principle there is a distinction between the two. Terrorism, in common with guerrilla war, is simply a mode of warfare; it carries no particular political baggage. In principle, anyone can do it, and for any set of motives. Insurgency, however, is a concept having considerable political content, and it constitutes by far the more serious menace to order and stability. None of the popular definitions are beyond challenge, but that offered by Krepinevich captures the heart of the matter well enough for our purposes: "An insurgency is a *protracted struggle* conducted methodically, step by step, in order to obtain specific intermediate objectives leading finally to the overthrow of the existing order."[49]

Krepinevich is unduly specific as to method, but he does highlight the point that an insurgency is all about an armed effort to effect revolutionary, at least radical and decisive, change. It is certain that terrorism will be one of the tactics employed by insurgents. But if an irregular enemy confines itself, or is compelled to be limited, to acts of terrorism, the threat that it poses to political stability is an order of magnitude less severe than is the menace from insurgency. Terrorism is an expensive and occasionally tragic nuisance for a society. But an organization that expresses its frustration, anger, and ambition solely by committing isolated outrages, is an organization that is going nowhere and can pose no real danger to a basically stable society. Needless to add, perhaps, if terrorists are to become insurgents, usually they need considerable assistance from what should be the forces of order. The struggle between terrorists and counterterrorists is very much a contest over legitimacy in the eyes of the public. For the purpose of this inquiry, it is useful and appropriate to treat insurgency and terrorism as comprising a single class of behavior, here termed irregular warfare.[50] What follows is a terse description of the character of the irregular warfare of insurgency and terrorism. Historical examples abound, but we are almost required to think principally of two major, and really unavoidable, cases in particular; Vietnam and Iraq 2003 to the present. I must emphasize that the intention here is not to shed new light on irregular warfare, for that subject is very well-understood indeed, at least in theory. Rather, the aim is to expose the key features of such warfare so that the depth of the challenge to the traditional American way of war can be assayed accurately.

Lest this analysis be accused of undue simplification, it recognizes that insurgency is not a simple, standard phenomenon. It follows that COIN must similarly adapt to the specific character of irregular challenge in question. An insurgency may move and breed among the people, the rural population in the Maoist model or urban dwellers in more advanced societies. Alternatively, and especially if it favors terrorist tactics, irregulars may devote little attention to political efforts at proselytization, placing their faith instead on the putative power of the violent deed. By military action, they intend to demonstrate the impotence of the government to provide protection. This *foco* theory of revolutionary warfare—focusing narrowly on violence per se—has a decidedly mixed record, as Che Guevara demonstrated all too personally in Bolivia in October 1967. Despite the wide range of terrorist-insurgent challenges, this author is persuaded that a single "working theory" of irregular warfare and how best to oppose it has sufficient integrity to deserve our confidence.

What do we know about countering the irregular warfare of insurgency and terrorism?

1. **Protect the People.** In COIN, the center of gravity is the people and their protection. The battlefield of most significance is the mind of the public. If people can be protected and believe they are protected, COIN is well on the way to success, if not outright victory. But to accord first priority to direct population protection is not a tactic that has wide appeal to a military establishment imbued with an aggressive spirit understandably reluctant to appear to surrender the initiative to the enemy.

2. **Intelligence Is King.** The key to operational advantage in COIN is timely, reliable intelligence. If COIN is to root out an insurgent-terrorist infrastructure, it must have information which can come only from the local public at large, or from defecting insurgents. Again, if the people feel that they are protected, that they have a good enough future with the established authorities, and that the authorities are going to win, the intelligence problem should solve itself. If insurgents lose in the minds of the people, they lose, period. With superior

intelligence, COIN wins. Insurgents or terrorists survive only by remaining elusive, by hiding in the sea of the people or in remote areas, which renders them ineffective. If the people can no longer be trusted to protect the terrorists' identities and safe houses, they cannot function safely. In short, a hostile public, or even just an unsympathetic one, translates as a social context nonpermissive for irregular warriors.

3. **Ideology Matters.** It is a general truth that every insurgency mobilizes around a political cause. There are apparent exceptions, as always, but typically insurgents rally to a potent idea, political or religious, or both. The insurgent action in Iraq from 2004 to the present appears to violate this principle, seeming in many cases to be driven more by a determination simply to ferment chaos than by any particular creed or vision of the just society. But the history of insurgency and COIN is quite unambiguous in its thoroughgoing validation of Clausewitz's insistence upon the political character of all military behavior.[51] Because COIN is, and can be explained as, a set of rules and techniques, as a method for winning an irregular conflict, the technique lends itself to being mistaken for the "victory kit." The French colonial army, for example, learned in Indochina what to do and what not to do against a revolutionary insurgent enemy. Educated by defeat in Southeast Asia and in the POW camps of the Viet Minh, thoughtful French paratroopers, legionnaires, and light infantrymen were ready to wage *la guerre moderne* in Algeria.[52] They waged modern war, which is to say irregular war, most effectively. Unfortunately for them, they failed to secure a firm intellectual grasp of the truth that war is a political act and that people are political animals. Tactical competence does not magically enable the counterinsurgent to manufacture an adequate political story. Modern war, French-style, could work tactically and operationally in Algeria, but never strategically. The reason was that the French military effort, no matter how tactically excellent and intellectually sophisticated, was always politically hollow. The French had, and could promise, no political idea with

a potent appeal to the Moslem populace. The COIN force must work in support of a credible, publicly attractive, political vision. That vision cannot be imposed from outside the society. More to the point, Western politicians, soldiers, and administrators, cannot "build nations," as the arrogant and absurd, but all too familiar, concept of "nation-building" suggests. As always, there will be an exception or two. If a country is utterly defeated and is occupied by the victor, then it is possible for political reconstruction to be effected, even in the face of an alien culture. One thinks of Japan after World War II. However, even in that case, much that is uniquely Japanese survived the cultural assault from abroad.

4. **The Irregular Enemy Is Not Usually the Target.** Since the battlefield in COIN is in people's minds and the protection of the people is the overriding priority, it follows that military plans for COIN should be radically different from those adopted for regular warfare. It would be a gross exaggeration to argue that insurgent forces are irrelevant, but that assertion, shocking to many conventional military minds, contains a vital verity. When success is possible, which is not always the case, COIN wins in the minds, and preferably the hearts (though just minds may well suffice), of a public that the COIN forces have persuaded will be protected and provided a better future. Victory will not be the product of engagements, even successful engagements, with insurgents, though military defeats will be damaging because they undermine the crucial protection story. If the irregular enemy is so foolish as to present itself in the open for mechanized destruction, so much the better, always provided the COIN elements do not waste whole neighborhoods in a ruthless quest to maximize the body count of suspected enemies. However, while an irregular war can be lost militarily, generally it cannot be won in that mode. If an insurgency is allowed to mature from Mao's second phase of guerrilla action into the third and final phase of open conventional combat, then indeed military events can prove conclusive. Nonetheless, from the point of view of COIN, the irregular enemy is more of a distraction than a focus for aggressive attention.

Insurgents and counterinsurgents are competing for the allegiance, or more often just the acquiescence, of the public. Actual combat between regular and irregular warriors has no strategic significance save with respect to the reputation of the belligerents in the eyes of the public, and with regard to the actual protection of the people. Contrary to traditional military practice, the objectives in COIN are neither the irregular enemy's forces, nor, with a vital reservation, the territory that they occupy and use. Insurgents' sanctuary areas are essential targets, because an irregular foe can be defeated logistically if it is forcibly deprived of reliable supply and intelligence and, as a result, is compelled to operate in ever closer proximity to the more heavily populated areas where the COIN forces should be deployed most extensively. That giant theorist of irregular warfare, Colonel Charles Callwell, writing a century ago about the lessons to be drawn from the colonial "small war" experiences of several imperial powers, averred as a central problem one which we need to treat with great reserve in the different conditions of today. He noted the near truism that "[i]t is the difficulty of bringing the foe to action which, as a rule, forms the most unpleasant characteristic of these wars [regulars against irregulars]."[53] Contrary to Callwell's message, however, this monograph maintains that determination to bring an elusive irregular enemy to battle more often than not proves to be a snare and a delusion. Victory, to repeat, is not won in COIN over the bodies of dead insurgents, probably not even if one imposes attrition on a Homeric scale.

5. **Unity of Effort.** Irregular warfare is, or at least should be, waged on both sides grand strategically. All of the instruments of persuasion, coercion, and influence need to be employed. The conflict will be political, ideological, economic, diplomatic, and military in several modes. The irregular enemy will not aspire to defeat the U.S. Army in battle, but it does not need to. If the Army strives to win a military victory, it will only exhaust itself, frustrate its domestic supporters, and dissipate its strengths chasing a chimera. To beat an insurgency, when

that is feasible, the COIN forces must organize and direct a strict unity of civilian and military effort with a single chain of command, and with political authority unambiguously in supreme command. While all warfare is political, irregular warfare is the most political of all, if one may be permitted to qualify an absolute. Military action has to be subordinated to political priorities. And, as we keep noting, the top priority must be the security of the majority of the population. The argument that the most effective way to protect people is to chase after their irregular tormentors, wherever they happen to be, simply does not work, attractive though it can sound. An analogy with piracy is false. Undoubtedly the superior solution to piracy was to take the initiative and attack the pirates at home. Unfortunately, few insurgencies provide the functional equivalents of pirates' lairs. For a better maritime analogy the introduction of convoying during World Wars I and II compelled the "pirate," that is, the submarine, to seek out civilian targets where they were protected. The experience of two world wars demonstrated conclusively that narrowly focused protection of the convoys per se rather than the conduct of aggressive hunting parties sweeping the seas looking for raiders, was the path to success. Parallel logic holds for the conduct of irregular warfare on land. To return to our theme, the focus must never shift from the true center of gravity of the struggle, the minds of the people. And COIN can succeed only when the military instrument is employed as part of a team that is led by political judgment and places its highest priority on real-time intelligence gathering from the public and solid police work. Of course, it is much easier to specify these desirables than it is to deliver them in practice.

6. **Culture Is Crucial.** In regular warfare between regular armies, the terms of engagement and character of military behavior will be so substantially similar as almost to warrant description as transcultural. The belligerents will share strengths and weaknesses in a tolerable common contemporary "grammar" of war, as Clausewitz expressed the matter.[54] Cultural differences will weigh in the balance,

as each side adapts ideas and equipment to suit its own circumstances, traditions, preferences, and service politics.[55] However, one can imagine a decisive military outcome to regular warfare achieved virtually regardless of the cultural differences between the protagonists. That is a deliberate slight exaggeration. It contrasts usefully with a condition of irregular warfare, of insurgency or pure terrorism. In the latter case, underappreciated differences in culture by a well-meaning but foreign COIN effort are near certain to prove fatal for the COIN enterprise. Culture refers to social capital. It means the beliefs, attitudes, habits of mind, and preferred ways of behavior of a social group. And, to repeat yet again, irregular wars are won or lost in the minds of the local people. If we do not understand what is in those minds, what they value and how much they value it, success secured against terrorists and other insurgents will most likely be only temporary.

Culture is crucial, both ours and theirs. "Theirs" for the obvious reason just outlined; restated, the local people decide who wins. "Ours" because we can approach and seek to understand other cultures only through the inevitably distorting prism of our own. The fact is that America is a proud, somewhat ideological, superpower, eager to spread and exert its "soft power" but prepared to apply the mailed fist of its hard power.[56] The very strength of Americans' cultural identity is both a blessing and a hindrance. On balance, as an ingredient in the potions prepared to reduce an insurgency, American culture is a barrier to understanding and effective behavior. To help offset the influence of what Americans cannot help being, which is to say, themselves, the armed forces have to be educated both formally and by the experience gained through direct local exposure. It should be needless to add that if the Army wages irregular warfare from a series of "Fort Apaches," isolated from the local people, not only does it look hostile, but it cannot acquire the familiarity with local opinion and mores that is so essential for success in COIN. American lives may be saved by fortification, but the strategic price is likely acceptance of a high risk of mission failure.

7. **No Sanctuaries and No External Support.** It is standard COIN doctrine to attempt to deny insurgents safe areas where they can rest, rally, regroup, recover, train, and whence they can sally forth at their discretion to wreak havoc. The sanctuaries may be protected by rugged natural terrain, complex urban terrain, or porous international frontiers. Every military, or quasi-military, effort requires a secure base area. COIN doctrine is correct to identify enemy sanctuaries as important targets. However, it must be apparent from our analysis that the key to defeating an insurgency cannot lie in the removal of sanctuaries, important though that must be. Indeed, there is some danger that a COIN effort could become so persuaded of the significance of sanctuary areas and assistance from abroad, and of the need to interdict the latter, that the truly decisive battlespace would be downgraded. To explain, if the COIN campaign is working well, irregulars' sanctuaries and foreign support will not much matter. The struggle will be won or lost not by harassing the irregulars' logistics, but rather by shaping the minds and convictions of the target people. Given an American way of war that stresses aggressive offensive action against enemy forces, sanctuaries and foreign supply lines will be tempting targets for the diversion of military effort to remote areas, probably far away from the centers of population.

8. **Time Is a Weapon.** Of all the many dimensions of strategy, time is the most intractable. Compensation for deficiencies elsewhere and corrections of errors are usually possible. But time lost is irrecoverable. The Western theory of war and strategy pays too little attention to war's temporal dimension. In particular, there is too little recognition that time itself can be a weapon. It can be used purposefully to compensate for material or other weakness, and to expose and stress the vulnerability of the enemy. In irregular warfare, the materially disadvantaged combatant is obliged to try to win slowly, for no other reason than he cannot win swiftly. When Americans

elect to participate in an irregular conflict, they need to know this. Also, they need to know that there may well be no practical, feasible way in which they can hasten a favorable outcome of a decisive military kind, an outcome that is all but certain to be unattainable. The insurgents will behave like the guerrillas described so poetically by T. E. Lawrence in his classic if overwritten theorizing in the piece "Guerrilla Warfare," where he describes guerrillas who attempt to deny our regulars worthwhile targets.[57]

As explained already, a well-educated COIN force will be relatively untroubled by the elusiveness of the irregular enemy. It will understand that the battle is won through gaining the confidence of the people the regulars can protect, not by the number of dead insurgent bodies that can be strewn across distant parts of the landscape. However, COIN is slow, can be tedious, will face setbacks, may well be challenged by less than ideal local political partners, and a host of other predictable difficulties. Most of the insurgents will be local, American COIN experts will not be. Americans will go home. The irregular enemy can win if it is able to outwait American patience, in the meantime creating insecurity and discouraging major reforms of a kind that should alter public attitudes. The mindset needed to combat an enemy who is playing a long game is not one that comes naturally to the American soldier or, for that matter, to the American public. To wage protracted war is not a preference in our military or strategic culture. Moreover, to accept the necessity for protraction is to tolerate terms of engagement dictated by the enemy; that is not an attractive fact to explain and defend to a doubting and increasingly impatient news media, public, and opposition party.

9. **Undercut the Irregular Enemy Politically.** While we will be tempted to demonize an irregular enemy, label him a terrorist or worse, the local people whose allegiance is the prize in the contest will have a more nuanced view.[58] They will know some of the insurgents, and they are certain to have some sympathy with some elements of the insurgents' political

story. Since successful COIN must speak convincingly to a public knowledgeable about local issues, including information on the character and motives of the insurgents, it is essential for us to demonstrate a mastery of local conditions in terms that resonate well locally.

There are many aspects to this rather general point about undercutting the irregular enemy politically. I will identify just two, adding them to the argument already made in favor of talking about the enemy in realistic, nondemonizing terms. First, given the protracted character of an irregular conflict, there should be time, if the political will is present, to address some of the political grievances that have fuelled the insurgency. This is not to suggest abject surrender to the nominal wish list of the enemy. But it is to claim that, more often than not, the insurgents are exploiting some quite genuine sources of public unrest. In its political dimension, a COIN strategy will seek to deprive the irregulars of their cause by co-opting it when feasible. To the extent to which that cannot or should not be done, the forces of order will need to demonstrate to the public that they offer a politically superior alternative of direct local benefit.

Second, a COIN campaign, and the local government that it is designed to assist, must behave within the law. The irregular enemy wishes to promote chaos, uncertainty, and overreaction by the forces of order. Success in COIN is measured by the scale of the public confidence that they can live in a land of law and order, wherein they need not fear for their personal security at the hands of anyone, official or other. It follows that when the government flouts its own laws, behaves arbitrarily, abuses detainees, and generally functions according to the principle of a very rough expediency, it does the insurgents' work for them. I cannot state often enough or clearly enough that victory or defeat in irregular warfare is all about the beliefs, attitudes, and consequent behavior of the public. Everything that an American COIN effort and its local allies do to combat the irregular enemy ultimately has strategic effect, positive or negative, upon the minds of that public. They are the stake, and they are the battlespace.

The discussion in this section of irregular warfare and its implications for COIN doctrine are not really controversial. However, what is problematic is the ability of the U.S. military, and the Army in particular, to adapt successfully to the character of the warfare described broadly above. Self-knowledge is essential if Americans are to address the challenge of irregular warfare with some good prospect of adapting successfully. In order to throw the pertinent realities into stark relief for clear appreciation, the next section presents an appreciation of the traditional American way of war, a way which in many respects still permeates American behavior. That American way of war is considered in light of the behavior needed for strategic effectiveness against irregular enemies.

The American Way of War Meets an Irregular Future.

The American way of war has been mentioned throughout this monograph, but has not been specified in an orderly and detailed way. This apparent neglect is explained by the fact that my primary mission has been to consider irregular warfare in strategic perspective. But now the several strands in this analysis come together as irregular enemies, and their modes of warfare, understood strategically, are considered as a challenge to the traditional American way of war. Of necessity, what follows is a personal characterization of the traditional, indeed cultural, American way of war. I specify 13 features, many of which can be qualified anecdotally by pointing out exceptions, but all of which I believe to be sound enough to stand as valid generalizations. Whereas a single exception must invalidate a scientific law (e.g., an apple that declines to obey the law of gravity), social scientific lore is far more tolerant of deviant cases. Rather than argue for each of my chosen features, I will restrict myself simply to explanation. It should be understood that no authoritative listing exists. Indeed, there could hardly be such, given that the notion of a national way of war is what we social scientists term an essentially contested concept.

The items pertain both to war as a whole and to its military conduct in warfare. At least three of the 13 features support the notion that the United States tends to confuse Principles of Warfare with Principles of War. If the country appreciated and generally adhered to a well-drafted and culturally-embedded set of Principles of War, principles that truly were Clausewitzian (and Sun-tzuan and Thucydidean), its strategic and political performance in conflict after conflict should be considerably improved.[59] But, for good or ill, Americans are what they are strategically. If, as I claim, Americans persist in failing to reap desired political rewards from their military efforts, even when the efforts themselves are largely successful, there are cultural, even structural, reasons why that is so. Most likely, Americans can remake their strategic performance only if they first remake their society, and that is a task beyond the ability of even the most optimistic agents of transformation. Moreover, one suspects that the strategic rewards would both disappoint and cost far too much in virtues sacrificed. Nonetheless, there is currently wholesale recognition in the armed forces of the seriousness and probable longevity of the menace posed by irregular enemies. It is at least possible that by deconstructing the standard American "way," and reviewing it from the perspective of countering irregulars, some pathways to improved performance may be identified. As always, though, first one must alert people to the problem.

1. Apolitical	8. Large-scale
2. Astrategic	9. Aggressive, offensive
3. Ahistorical	10. Profoundly regular
4. Problem-solving, optimistic	11. Impatient
5. Culturally challenged	12. Logistically excellent
6. Technology dependent	13. Highly sensitive to casualties
7. Focused on firepower	

Characteristics of the American Way of War.

1. **Apolitical.** Americans are wont to regard war and peace as sharply distinct conditions. The U.S. military has a long history of waging war for the goal of victory, paying scant regard to the consequences of the course of its operations for the character of the peace that will follow. Civilian policymakers have been the ones primarily at fault. In war after war they have tended to neglect the Clausewitzian dictum that war is about, and only about, its political purposes. Characteristically, though certainly not invariably, U.S. military efforts have not been suitably cashed in the coin of political advantage.[60] The

traditional American separation of politics and the conduct of war is a lethal weakness when dealing with irregular enemies. Irregular conflict requires a unity of effort by all the instruments of grand strategy, and it must be guided by a unified high command. In that high command, the political authority has to be paramount. As a general rule, there can be no military solution to the challenge posed by irregulars. The principle task of the soldier is to provide the security without which decisive political progress is impossible.

2. **Astrategic.** Strategy is, or should be, the bridge that connects military power with policy. When Americans wage war as a largely autonomous activity, leaving worry about peace and its politics to some later day, the strategy bridge has broken down. The conduct of war cannot be self-validating. For a premier example of this malady, one must cite Vietnam. For example, the United States sought to apply its new-found theory of limited war in an ill-crafted effort to employ modulated, on-off-on coercion by air bombardment to influence Hanoi in favor of negotiations.[61] To resort to Clausewitzian terms again, while war has its policy logic, it also has its own "grammar."[62] It is prudent to take notice of these words of wisdom from Samuel Huntington: "Military forces are not primarily instruments of communication to convey signals to an enemy; they are instead instruments of coercion to compel him to alter his behavior."[63]

    Excellence in strategy has not been an American strength, at least not since George Washington defeated the British strategically. The reasons why Americans talk a lot about strategy, but understand it a lot less and practice it rarely, do not really concern us in this monograph. Suffice it to say that the major causes of the problem are twofold: a longstanding tradition of material superiority which offers few incentives for strategic calculation; and the nation's traditional theory of civil-military relations, which discourages probing dialogue between policymaker and soldier. Unfortunately, the terrorist and the insurgent are probably functioning strategically. Indeed, they can hope to succeed in no other way. As we have commented already, such irregulars are playing a long game. Their tactical behavior is of little, if any, inherent significance. They do not plan and execute would-be decisive military actions; COIN is a quintessentially strategic struggle. Everything that is done by both sides potentially has political implications. This is not exactly a deep insight. What I have just stated is nothing more than Clausewitz's definition of strategy. A United States that does not really "do strategy," at least not for long, because it does not truly understand it, will be outfought and out-thought by irregular enemies who *must* "do strategy" if they are to survive and prosper.

3. **Ahistorical.** As a future-oriented, still somewhat "new" country, one that has a founding ideology of faith in, hope for, and commitment to, human betterment, it is only to be expected that Americans should be less than highly respectful of what they might otherwise be inclined to allow history to teach them. A defense community led by the historically disrespectful and ill-educated, is all but condemned to find itself surprised by events for which some historical understanding could have prepared them. History cannot repeat itself, of course, but, as naval historian Geoffrey Till has aptly observed, "The chief utility of history for the analysis of present and future lies in its ability, not to point out lessons, but to isolate things that need thinking about. . . . History provides insights and questions, not answers."[64]

As Sam Sarkesian, John Collins, and Max Boot, among others, have sought to remind us, the United States has a rich and extensive history of experience with irregular enemies.[65] Moreover, that experience was by no means entirely negative. The trouble was and, until very recently, has remained, that such varied experience of irregular warfare was never embraced and adopted by the Army as the basis for the development of doctrine for a core competency. Rephrased, the Army improvised and waged irregular warfare, sometimes just regular war against irregulars, when it had to. But that task was always viewed officially as a regrettable diversion from preparation for "real war." Real war, of course, meant war against regular peers, the kind of war that Europeans waged against each other.

To be brutal, the U.S. Army has a fairly well-filled basket of negative experience with irregular enemies. If the institution is willing to learn, and to regard COIN as a necessary enduring competency to be achieved through an adaptable transformation, past errors all but demand to be recognized. As we have sought to insist throughout this monograph, COIN warfare is not a black art. Rather, its principles and priorities are well-known and noncontroversial. All that is necessary is for the soldier to be willing and able to learn from history, recent American history at that. Unfortunately, the first and truest love of the U.S. defense community is with technology, not with history. That great American strategic theorist, Bernard Brodie, explained for all time why history should not be neglected. He reminded those in need of reminding that "the only empirical data we have about how people conduct war and behave under its stresses is our experience with it in the past, however much we have to make adjustments for subsequent changes in conditions."[66] An Army struggling to adapt to the unfamiliar and unwelcome challenges of irregular warfare cannot afford to be ahistorical, let alone antihistorical.

4. **Problem-solving and Optimistic**. Holding to an optimistic public culture characterized by the belief that problems can always be solved, the American way in war is not easily discouraged or deflected once it is exercised with serious intent to succeed. That is to say, not when the American way is manifested in such anti-strategic sins against sound statecraft as the "drive-by" cruise missile attacks of the late 1990s. The problem-solving faith, the penchant for the engineering fix, has the inevitable consequence of leading U.S. policy, including its use of armed force, to attempt the impossible.[67] After all, American history is decorated triumphantly with "impossible" achievements, typically against physical geography. Conditions are often misread as problems. Conditions have to be endured, perhaps ameliorated, and

generally tolerated, whereas problems, by definition, can be solved.

There are two ways in which an American way of war imbued with a problem-solving spirit is apt to stray from the path of strategic effectiveness. First, irregular enemies, terrorist-insurgents, are not usefully regarded as problems to be solved. As we have observed already, these irregulars are waging a protracted war, eschewing the kind of open engagements that might just produce a clear-cut military decision. Since the irregular foe cannot be brought to battle en masse, he is not a problem that the Army can solve tactically or operationally. Instead, following classic COIN doctrine, the problem of the insurgent is best treated as a condition that has to be addressed indirectly, as security is provided for, and hopefully the trust is gained of, the local people. That has to be a slow, gradual process. If one does not understand that and act accordingly, one has no future in COIN.

5. **Culturally-challenged.** Belatedly, it has become fashionable to berate the cultural insensitivity that continues to hamper American strategic performance.[68] Bear in mind American public ideology, with its emphasis on political and moral uniqueness, manifest destiny, divine mission even, married to the multidimensional sense of national greatness. Such self-evaluation has not inclined Americans to be especially respectful of the beliefs, habits, and behavior of other cultures. This has been, and continues to be, especially unfortunate in the inexorably competitive field of warfare. From the Indian Wars on the internal frontier, to Iraq and Afghanistan today, the American way of war has suffered from the self-inflicted damage growing out of a failure to understand the enemy of the day. For a state that now accepts, indeed insists upon, a global mandate to act as sheriff, this lack of cultural empathy, including a lack of sufficiently critical self-knowledge, is most serious.

There is no mode of warfare, conducted in any geographical environment, wherein the enemy's strategic culture is of no importance. Even in the most extreme of warfare's technological forms, a large-scale "exchange" of nuclear weapons between super or great powers, the firing and targeting doctrine of the foe will not be innocent of cultural influence. Nuclear doctrines will express calculations of military and geostrategic realities, calculations conducted by encultured strategists. Through much of the 1970s and 1980s, U.S. nuclear strategy carried some promise of damage limitation for America only if Soviet nuclear strategy reciprocated in targeting restraint. Soviet attitudes towards war, including nuclear war, were of vital importance. Since culture was, indeed still is, a significant dimension of warfare with nuclear weapons, how much more salient must it be in irregular conflict. Recall that the battlespace in the fight against insurgents and terrorists is in the minds of the people whose allegiance or acquiescence is the stake in the struggle. In COIN, the Army needs to engage and stay engaged with the people who need protection, not with the irregular enemy. That enemy will face inevitable defeat if the Army is accepted as a friendly guardian, and the people are willing to back the political future promised by the government.

It hardly needs emphasizing that to win the trust of the people at risk requires a measure of comprehension of their beliefs, their hopes and fears, their recent history — in short, their culture. To acquire such cultural empathy is no simple matter. It cannot be achieved from inside "Fort Apache," nor can it be gained by occasional energetic and violent sweeps through "bandit country."

6. **Technology-dependent.** The exploitation of machinery is the American way of war. One may claim that airpower is virtually synonymous with that way of war, and that its employment as the leading military instrument of choice has become routine. So at least it appeared in the 1990s, during the warm afterglow of airpower's triumph in the First Gulf War.[69] America is the land of technological marvels and of extraordinary technology dependency. It was so from early in the 19th century when a shortage of skilled craftsmen — they had tended to remain in Europe — obliged Americans to invent

and use machines as substitutes for human skill and muscle. Necessity bred preference and then excellence, and the choice of mechanical solutions assumed a cultural significance that has endured. The watershed, unsurprisingly, was the experience of the Civil War. The way of war that succeeded in that most bloody of America's struggles was logistical, having been enabled by an exploitation of raw industrial power that foreign observers found awesome. American soldiers say that the human being matters most, but, in practice, the American way of war, past, present, and prospectively future, is quintessentially and uniquely technology-dependent. The Army's transformation plans are awash with prudent words on the many dimensions of future conflict, but at its core lies a drive to acquire an exceedingly expensive Future Combat System, consisting of a network of vital technologies.[70]

Given the range of potential demands that foreign policy may place on the Army, the only sound plan for the future has to be one that is flexible and adaptable. The enemies of tomorrow are at least as likely to take regular as irregular forms. The issue is not technology, nor is it any particular set of weapons and support systems. Instead, the difficulty lies in the fact that the American armed forces are culturally attuned to favoring technological solutions over other approaches, while irregular enemies pose problems of a kind where technology typically offers few real advantages. Indeed, machines and dependence upon them are apt to have negative value, because although they can save some American lives, they tend to isolate American soldiers from the social, and even the military, context which is the decisive battleground in irregular conflict. Contrary to appearances, perhaps, this is to condemn neither machines nor technology in principle. Whatever technology can do that is useful in COIN and for counterterrorism certainly should be done. It is the use, or misuse through overuse, of technology that is at issue, not technology itself. The experience of several countries demonstrates unambiguously that there is no correlation between technical sophistication and success in the conduct of warfare against irregulars.[71] Remember the proposed "McNamara Fence" during the Vietnam War and suchlike extravagant follies.

7. **Focused on Firepower.** General Westmoreland, then Commander of MACV, once famously and characteristically told a press conference that the correct approach to counterinsurgency was "firepower."[72] It has long been the American way in warfare to send metal in harm's way in place of vulnerable flesh. This admirable expression of the country's machine-mindedness undoubtedly is the single most characteristic feature of American war-making at the sharp end. Needless to say, perhaps, a devotion to firepower, while defensible, indeed necessary, cannot help encouraging the armed forces to rely on it even when other modes of military behavior would be more suitable. In irregular conflicts in particular, heavy and sometimes seemingly indiscriminate, certainly disproportionate, resort to firepower solutions, readily becomes self-defeating. A focus on firepower as the key to a victory defined in classic military terms produces the attitude that what we do in war is service targets. Instead of being considered in his cultural context, the enemy is reduced to the dehumanized status of the object of U.S. firepower.[73] At its nadir, this characteristic was demonstrated in action in Vietnam with the prevalence of the U.S. artillery's very extensive practice of conducting unaimed harassment and interdiction fire.[74] A notable fraction of that artillery fire was expended for no better reason than that the ammunition was available in embarrassing abundance.

Regular warfare is composed of ever varying mixes of the eternal trinity of fire, movement, and shock. Irregular warfare, however, is different. There can be no decisive military engagement, because an agile, elusive, and competent irregular enemy will decline to expose himself in such a way that he can be obliterated by fire, outmaneuvered to annihilation, or destroyed physically and morally by shock effect. In COIN the rules of engagement broadly are the reverse of those standard in regular combat. When in doubt, one should not fire. Why? Because as a general rule, COIN must be conducted around the civilian population who comprise the center of gravity of the conflict. Trigger-happiness cannot help producing undesirable collateral damage; in other words, dead and wounded civilians and fear of American military behavior. Better that an insurgent should escape or, dare one say it, that an American or allied soldier or official be killed, than that a dozen or so bystanders pay the price for being in the wrong place at the wrong time. The kind of disciplined self-restraint in the resort to force that is mandatory for success in warfare against irregulars does not come easily or naturally to young people whom we train to be aggressive and to kill when necessary in self-defense. Nor does it come easily to officers who have well-founded anxieties about the career implications of suffering casualties. If the armed forces are serious about supporting policy with high competency in the conduct of war against irregulars, then they will need to curb their traditional, indeed cultural, excessive love affair with firepower.

8. **Large-scale.** As a superpower, the United States tends to excel at enterprises conducted on a scale that matches its total assets. Professor Huntington believes, at least he believed in 1985, that "the United States is a big country, and we should fight wars in a big way."[75] More controversially, he claimed that "[b]igness not brains is our advantage, and we should exploit it."[76] No doubt those words will irritate and anger many readers. However, there is an important self-awareness in Huntington's point. As a large rich country, for the better part of 200 years the United States has waged its many wars, regular and irregular, domestic and foreign, as one would expect of a society that is amply endowed materially. Poor societies are obliged to wage war frugally. They have no choice other than to attempt to fight smarter than their rich enemies. The United States has been blessed with wealth in all its forms. Inevitably, the armed forces, once mobilized and equipped, have fought a rich person's war. They could hardly do otherwise. From the time of the Civil War, foreign observers

have been astonished by the material generosity with which American troops have been supplied and equipped. Strategic necessity is the mother of military invention, and since the 1860s, at least, Americans have had little need to invent clever work-arounds for material lack. It is not self-evident that the United States is able to wage war in a materially minimalist fashion, any more than that today's volunteer soldiers and their families would tolerate campaign conditions marked by what would be regarded as unnecessary discomfort. The American Army at war is American society at war. This is not so much a problem as a condition.

True, Americans have at times waged modern war on a shoestring, and the experience was predictably unhappy. Anyone wondering how Americans perform when the material balance is not weighted heavily in their favor will not be short of historical evidence. They could do worse than study the campaign on Guadalcanal in the second half of 1942, or, for another grim classic, the fate of Task Force Smith in Korea in July 1950.[77] These, however, were exceptions to the rule that because the United States was the world's greatest industrial nation, it waged its industrial-age warfare on a scale that others could not hope to match. But because the American way of war traditionally had to be unleashed only after a surge of emergency and time-consuming mobilization, the cost was apt to be heavy for the soldiers at the sharp end. To "come as you are with what you have got" is ever a bloody and extraordinarily dangerous duty. The implications of America's excellence in the conduct of warfare on the large scale for its ability to combat irregular enemies are mixed, but on balance probably have been negative. Warfare against a lightly armed irregular foe short of numbers is not simply a somewhat scaled-down version of warfare as usual. The American strategic cultural trait of "bigness," of functioning with large footprints, is apt to be counterproductive. In COIN, the more evident the American presence and influence, the less legitimate and competent the local authorities must appear to be. The larger the American military contribution, particularly if its soldiers look hostile and behave as if they are in bandit country, the more the U.S. presence will resemble an occupation.[78] American culture, in all senses of the term, is a powerful force, particularly in its hold on Americans. Large numbers of Americans, being Americans, acting like Americans, and indeed living in cultural and social facsimiles of America in an alien society, amount to a challenge, or insult, to local mores. This is a necessary consequence of the injection of large numbers of Americans, with all the logistics deemed essential to the American way of life that the volunteer soldier expects, into the midst of an alien cultural milieu. Of course, Americans can reduce their visibility by retreating into fortified bunkers or by deploying away from heavily populated areas. To behave thus, however, is to operate in a manner counterproductive for irregular warfare, where the battlefield, as we keep insisting, is the people.

9. **Aggressive and Offensive.** Geopolitics, culture, and material endowment have combined to pull the American way of war towards an aggressive offensive style. Geopolitically viewed, the United States is effectively insular, albeit on a continental scale. Not since the War of 1812 has the country faced a serious threat in North America except, of course, from its slave-holding states in 1861-65. Because of America's geopolitical isolation, a product of geography and culture, in the 20th century the country repeatedly joined in wars that already were well underway. America had to take the initiative and move men and material across oceans. Also, it was obliged to commit to offensive operations in order to take back the gains made by enemies in Europe and Asia at the outset of their rampages of conquest. U.S. political motives may have been broadly defensive. But as was the case with Iraq's seizure of Kuwait in 1990, the principal guardian of the status quo, the United States, had no military choice other than aggressive offensive action. More often than not, an aggressor is content to take his prize and then offer an armistice and a conference to bless the crimes just committed. Prior to the creation of NATO and the subsequent U.S. commitment to maintain a substantial garrison in Europe, the American strategic role

in Eurasia was notably episodic. With the exception of the nuclear-shadowed Cold War of 1947-89, a historical anomaly, when an American army is sent across an ocean its society expects it to do something important. There are many plausible explanations for the offensive preference in the American way of war; we will cite some of the more significant among them. In summary form, an aggressive offensive style:

- is required if decisive victory is to be achieved against enemies who have to be ejected from ill-gotten gains, or otherwise taught the error of their ways;

- is mandated by a domestic political context that regards American participation in war as so extraordinary an event that it has to be completed as rapidly as possible, so that a condition of peace and normalcy can be restored;

- is fitting because the United States fights only against evil regimes, and is not disposed to wage limited wars for limited political purposes, save under duress, as in Korea, 1950-53.

- is appropriate to America's strength and strengths. The United States is obliged to develop forces that are highly mobile. In a sense, the conquest of distance has been America's strategic history;

- has a record of success. It is difficult to argue with a history that appears to validate the military merits of an offensive style.

- via a succession of sometimes parallel offensive operations was the American way, briefly in 1918, and then of geopolitical necessity in 1942-45.

The American way of war can be traced back to the 18th century, if not earlier, but this monograph will content itself with noting that the illustrative apogee of that "way" occurred during World War II. America had demonstrated to observers around the globe a way of war that delivered decisive military victory. That way favored mobility, movement (not necessarily skillful maneuver), command of "the commons" (the high seas and the air), and firepower. Americans sought to take war to the enemy, as rapidly and destructively as the machines of industrial age warfare permitted. The American way was truly awesome in its ability to kill people and break things. The problem today is that if the country's strategic future is going to be plagued more and more by challenges posed by irregular enemies, America's soldiers will lack enemy targets for their traditionally preferred style of operation. As we have maintained repeatedly, COIN warfare demotes the irregular enemy to the status of a secondary objective. Aggressive offensive action against an enemy of uncertain location and identity is more likely to wreak political damage upon the COIN endeavor, a self-inflicted wound, than upon the enemy. Naturally, there is a time and place for offensive action. But, as the dominant characteristic of the official style of war, offensive action is likely to prove counterproductive against irregular enemies in many, perhaps most, circumstances. This is not to deny that irregular targets of opportunity certainly should be pursued aggressively if the enemy is foolish enough to expose himself for discrete destruction. Also, it is emphatically true that America's future strategic history is not going to be populated wholly by enemies of an irregular kind, no matter how fashionable that belief may be today.

10. **Profoundly Regular.** Few, if any, armies have been equally competent in the conduct of regular and irregular warfare. The U.S. Army is no exception to that rule. Both the Army and the Marine Corps have registered occasional successes in irregular warfare, while individual Americans have proved themselves adept at the conduct of guerrilla warfare.[79] As institutions, however, the U.S. armed forces have not been friendly either to irregular warfare or to their own would-be practitioners and advocates of what was regarded as the sideshow of unconventional warfare or counterinsurgency.[80] American soldiers have been overwhelmingly regular in their view of, approach to, and skill in, warfare. They have always prepared near exclusively for "real war," which is to say combat against a tolerably symmetrical, regular enemy. Irregular warfare — or low-intensity conflict (LIC) as denominated by the inclusive

and therefore vague 1960s term-of-art[81] — has been regarded as a lesser but included class of challenge. In other words, a good regular army has been assumed to be capable of turning its strengths to meet irregular enemies, whereas the reverse would not be true. It has not generally been appreciated that LIC is not simply a scaled-down version of "real war," but requires an entirely different mindset, doctrine, and training.

The United States has a storehouse of first-hand historical experience which should educate its soldiers in the need to recognize that regular and irregular warfare are significantly different. That educational process still has a distance to travel, but it will travel nowhere without steady endorsement from senior leadership, which appears to be forthcoming at present. Anyone in need of persuasion as to the extent of the regularity of the mindset dominant in America's military institutions need look no further than to the distinctly checkered history of the country's Special Operations Forces (SOF), as we observed earlier.

America's SOF have endured a Cinderella existence. They have prospered somewhat with episodic civilian political sponsorship, but not until very recent times have they been regarded and treated as an important element in the combined arms team. In the 1960s, for example, notwithstanding the enthusiasm of some "new frontiersmen" for the green berets in COIN, SOF efforts were accommodated all too well within the conventional grand designs of MACV.[82] Also, in Vietnam and since, there is some tension between SOF as the expert practitioners of unconventional warfare, and SOF in the local liaison and training roles so vital for COIN. Even a very regular military mind can be attracted to SOF if their assigned tasks are aggressive offensive actions undertaken on a very small scale. In other words, some special operations can appear simply to be scaled-down versions of the traditional American style in war.

The SOF are America's irregular regulars. How they are permitted to operate, and how well or poorly their duties fit into a comprehensive grand design for COIN, for example, tell us how far America's regular military establishment has moved towards incorporating an irregular instrument in its toolkit.[83] The jury is still out on whether today, really for the first time, the armed forces will succeed in making doctrinal and operational sense of their invaluable special warriors. On one hand, historical experience inclines one to be skeptical, but on the other, never before has the country elevated irregular enemies to the status of the dominant threat of an era.

11. **Impatient.** America is an exceptionally ideological society and, to date at least, it has distinguished clearly between conditions of peace and war. Americans have approached warfare as a regrettable occasional evil that has to be concluded as decisively and rapidly as possible. That partially moral perspective has not always sat well with the requirements of a politically effective use of force. For example, an important reason why MACV was not impressed by the promise of dedicated, time-proven counterinsurgency techniques in Vietnam, was the undeniable fact that such a style of warfare was expected to take far too long to show major results. Furthermore, America's regular military minds, and the domestic public, have been schooled to expect military action to produce conclusive results. At Khe Sahn in 1968, for a case in point, MACV was searching for an ever elusive decisive victory. As a consequence, it was lured into remote terrain , far from the cities where the vast majority of the people had congregated. The nationwide popular rising (wich never came) was planned and expected by Hanoi to be an urban event, with a little help from the VC, of course. Today, cultural bias towards swift action for swift victory is amplified by mass news media that are all too ready to report a lack of visible progress as evidence of stalemate and error.

Impatience is always a military vice, but never is this more true than in the conduct of war against irregular enemies. Those enemies have to use time as a weapon. We cannot claim we have not been warned. The rationale for, character, and structure of protracted war was described in ample detail 70 years ago by Mao Tse-tung; with local variants, it has been practiced around the world ever since by insurgents of many political persuasions.[84] It is probably no exaggeration to claim that a campaign plan fuelled by impatience must prove fatal to the prospects for success in irregular warfare. An impatient combatant literally will be seeking to achieve the impossible. Unless the irregular makes a truly irreversible political error, swift and decisive success against him, let alone some facsimile of victory, simply is not attainable. The center of gravity in irregular warfare, which is to say the local people and their allegiance, cannot be seized and held by dramatic military action. Against irregular foes, America's soldiers, and more particularly America's local allies, must be prepared to play a long game. The Army knows this, but whether the American body politic shares in this enlightenment is much less certain. It may be important for this analysis to repeat here a point advanced earlier. Americans are right to be uneasy about open-ended military commitments to allies who are struggling against insurgencies. There is much to be said for U.S. forces to devote most of their distinctive strengths to keeping the fight fair for our local friends. This may well require the taking of suitably violent action, certainly the issuing of some fearsome threats, against foreign backers of an insurgency. But terrorists and other insurgents ultimately can be worn down and overcome only by local initiatives and steady effort, not by American COIN behavior, no matter how expertly conducted. As a general rule, to which there will always be the odd exceptions, irregular wars cannot be won by foreigners, regardless of their good intentions and the high quality of their means and methods. Such high-quality methods are, of course, greatly to be desired, and would stand in healthy contrast with much of America's record in countering irregular enemies over the past 50 years.

12. **Logistically Excellent.** American history is a testament to the need to conquer distance. Americans at war have been exceptionally able logisticians. With a continental-size interior and an effectively insular geostrategic location, such ability has been mandatory if the country was to wage war at all, let alone wage it effectively. Recalling the point that

virtues can become vices, it can be argued that America not infrequently has waged war more logistically than strategically, which is not to deny that in practice the two almost merge, so interdependent are they.[85] The efficient support of the sharp end of American war-making can have, and has had, the downside of encouraging a tooth-to-tail ratio almost absurdly weighted in favor of the latter. A significant reason why firepower has been, and remains, the long suit in the American way of war, is that there repeatedly has been an acute shortage of soldiers in the infantry. A large logistical footprint, and none come larger than the American, requires a great deal of guarding, helps isolate American troops from local people and their culture, and tends to grow as it were organically in what has been pejoratively called the "logistical snowball."[86] Given that logistics is the science of supply and movement, America's logistical excellence, with its upside and its downside, of necessity has rested upon mastery of "the commons." Borrowing from Alfred Thayer Mahan, who wrote of the sea as a "wide common," Barry Posen has explained how and why the United States is master not only of the wide common of the high seas of Mahan's time, but also of the new commons of the air, space, and cyberspace.[87] Should this mastery cease to be assured, the country would have difficulty waging war against all except Mexicans and Canadians.

Those who might doubt the historical reality of a distinctive American way of war are hereby invited to compare with other countries the amount of materiel and the quantity and quality of support deemed essential to keep American soldiers tolerably content in the field. Many critics of General Westmoreland's strategy in Vietnam failed to notice that he was always painfully short of fighting soldiers. The U.S. military presence under his command may have totaled some 550,000, but no more than 80,000 of those soldiers were "fighting men."[88] There is a crossover point where logistical sufficiency, in any kind of war, regular or irregular, can slip into an excess that is counterproductive. In regular warfare, the traditional American way provides the infrastructure and depth of materiel that permit sustained combat. By way of the sharpest of contrasts, for example, Hitler's Luftwaffe was always in more or less desperate straits because of a lack of spare parts. In World War II, both Germany and Japan fielded flashy "shop window" forces that lacked staying power. The American way is the reverse of that. But in the conduct of irregular warfare, which almost invariably is waged on foreign soil, America's traditional way with abundant goods and services for the troops does have a rather obvious downside. The American logistical footprint is heavy, and it grows organically. The American way of war entails large bases that require protection. Those bases, dumps, and other facilities help isolate Americans from the local people and their culture, and, indeed, they create a distinct economy which signals the political fact that America has taken over. Naturally, it is difficult to envisage serious measures to lighten the logistical footprint, given concerns about reenlistment, political pressures from soldiers' relatives, and soldier-citizens' notions of their rights. To succeed in COIN in particular, as it has been discussed in this monograph, the Army needs to adapt in the direction of lighter, more agile forces, a process that is already underway. Furthermore, in gauging the extent of its material necessities in the field, it should give far greater weight to the irregular perspective than has been the case heretofore.

13. **Highly Sensitive to Casualties.** In common with the Roman Empire, the American guardian of world order is much averse to suffering a high rate of military casualties, and for at least one of the same reasons. Both superstates had and have armies that are small, too small in the opinion of many, relative to their responsibilities. Moreover, well-trained professional soldiers, volunteers all, are expensive to raise, train, and retain, and are difficult to replace. Beyond the issue of cost-effectiveness, however, lies the claim that American society has become so sensitive to casualties that it is no longer tolerant of potentially bloody ventures in muscular foreign governance. The most careful recent sociological research suggests that this popular notion about the American way of war, that it must seek

to avoid American casualties at almost any price, has been exaggerated.[89] Nonetheless, exaggerated or not, it is a fact that the United States has been perfecting a way in warfare that is expected, even required, to result in very few casualties for the home team. U.S. commanders certainly have operated since the Cold War under strict orders to avoid losses. The familiar emphasis upon force protection as "job one," virtually regardless of the consequences for the success of the mission, is a telling expression of this cultural norm. September 11, 2001, went some way towards reversing the apparent trend favoring, even demanding, friendly casualty avoidance. Culture, after all, does change with context. As quoted earlier, the *National Defense Strategy* document of March 2005 opens with the uncompromising declaration, "America is a nation at war." For so long as Americans believe this to be true, the social context for military behavior should be far more permissive of casualties than was the case in the 1990s. Both history and common sense tell us that Americans will tolerate casualties, even high casualties, if they are convinced both that the political stakes are vital, and that the government is trying hard to win. It must be noted, though, that Americans have come to expect an exceedingly low casualty rate because that has been their recent experience. That expectation has been fed by events, by the evolution of a high-technology way in warfare that exposes relatively few American soldiers to mortal danger, and by the low quality of recent enemies. When the context allows, it is U.S. military style to employ machines rather than people and to rely heavily on firepower to substitute for a more dangerous mode of combat for individuals. A network-centric Army, if able to afford the equipment, carries the promise of being supported by even more real-time on-call firepower than is available today.

If the United States is serious about combating irregular enemies in a way that stands a reasonable prospect of success, it will have to send its soldiers into harm's way to a degree that could promote acute political discomfort. The all-service defense transformation mandated by the Office of the Secretary of Defense is very much a high-technology voyage into the future. The focus is on machines, and the further exploitation of the computer in particular. Overall, it is not unfair to observe that this transformation, with its promise of even better performance in Command, Control, Communications, Computers, Information/Intelligence, Surveillance, Targeting and Reconnaissance (C^{4}ISTAR), should strengthen the American ability to wage its traditional style of war. Enemies, once detected, will be tracked and then obliterated by stand-off firepower, much of it delivered from altitude. American soldiers will see little of the foe in the flesh, and civilians will be protected from suffering as victims of collateral damage, to some degree at least, by the precision with which America's forces will be able to direct their fire. A major attraction of this style of war is that few Americans will be at risk. The problem is that such a technology-dependent, stand-off style is not appropriate for the conduct of war against irregulars, except in special cases. Certainly it is not suitable as the principal mode of operation. Irregular warfare is different, as we must keep insisting. For American soldiers to be useful in COIN, they have to be deployed "up close and personal" vis-à-vis the people who are the stake in the struggle. The more determinedly the Army strives to avoid casualties by hiding behind fortifications and deploying with armored protection, the less likely is it to be effective in achieving the necessary relationship of trust with the people. Of course, there will be circumstances when insurgents escalate violence in urban terrain in an endeavor to tempt Americans to fight back in their preferred style with profligate resort to firepower. In stressful circumstances, it may be hard to remember that in COIN dead insurgents are not proof of success, any more than home-side casualty avoidance by us is such proof.

Conclusions.

Early in this monograph I expressed my thinking with a three-pointed argument. By way of conclusion, we will revisit those claims, with a particular view to drawing together the diverse threads of irregular enemies and warfare, strategy, and the American way of war. Where appropriate, recommendations intended to help the Army meet irregular challenges more effectively will be suggested.

The first conclusion of this monograph is that war and strategy have, indeed must have, constant natures throughout history and with respect to politically motivated violence in all modes. It necessarily follows that we need only a single theory to uncover the secrets of war and strategy. One can stumble upon foolish references to a post-Clausewitzian era, or a pre-Clausewitzian period. Be not misled. The great Prussian, with his unfinished theory of war, is more than good enough to apply to all periods and all brands of nastiness. However, in common with Clausewitz and, one must say, the dictates of common sense, I recognize fully that the characteristics of war evolve, and that different wars in the same period will have distinctive features. Furthermore, the main elements that comprise the unchanging nature of war—passion, chance, reason, danger, exertion, uncertainty, and friction—though always present, must vary in their relative effect. To some degree, but only to *some* degree, they may be controllable.

I affirmed the merit of the hypothesis that strategy does indeed have an essence. If there is a single idea which best captures that essence, it is *instrumentality*. So long as one never forgets that strategy is about the consequences of the use of force and the threat of its use, and not about such use itself, one will keep to the straight and narrow. That having been said, a sound grasp of strategy's essence offers no protection, or at most only inadequate protection, against foolish policy or military failure. In the latter regard, it is worth quoting one of my favorite theorists again, Colonel Charles Callwell of the British Army, who wrote in his justly famous book, *Small Wars*, 100 years ago, "Strategy is not, however, the final arbiter in war. The battle-field decides, and on the battle-field the advantage passes over to the regular army."[90] He had just been explaining how the irregular enemy in colonial warfare typically enjoyed a strategic advantage. His point was that strategic advantage is all very well, but ultimately the troops, regular or irregular, have to be able to fight well. The good Colonel was not entirely correct, but we can hardly criticize him for not foreseeing the extensive politicization of irregular warfare in the 20th century.[91] He did not anticipate a strategic context wherein the battlefield lay in the minds of the local people.

Although irregular warfare in all its modes is different from regular combat in many respects, it is not at all distinctive from the perspective of the essence of strategy. War is war, and strategy is strategy. There are no "new" wars and "old" wars, no "Third Generation Wars" and "Fourth Generation Wars." There are only wars.[92] Strategy, in its essence, works identically for regular and for irregular belligerents, and in regular and irregular warfare. The characteristics of different forms of war and styles in warfare will vary widely, but there is a common currency in strategic effect, no matter how that effect is generated. We can appreciate that tactical, even operational, excellence, in the waging of irregular war, or indeed any kind of war, must be at a severe discount, a waste, if it is not directed by a constant concern for its strategic effect upon the course of political events. The logic of strategy is the same for wars of all kinds, even though the styles and tools of combat will differ.

It is important for the Army to understand the linkages and interdependencies among strategy, operations, and tactics. There is some value in the concept of strategic land power. The term reminds us that what soldiers do has strategic effect. Since that strategic effect has political consequences, soldiers should appreciate that their tactical behavior is permeated with political meaning. To make such a claim risks affronting an American tradition that asserts a separation of war from politics, but that view was never sound or sustainable, and therefore could not be practical.

The second conclusion of this monograph is that the United States has a persisting strategy deficit, which reflects a political deficit, in its approach to war in all its forms. To put this conclusion in context, we have argued that the United States has an enduring way of war which deserves characterization as cultural. It is possible that the contemporary drive for military transformation may be hindered, even partially frustrated, by American public, strategic, and military culture. The current crop of official documents on transformation may be too optimistic in their aspirations for American military cultural change. Understandably, those documents are not eloquent on the question of the country's competence in strategy.

An American strategy deficit is, of course, a weakness which renders the Army a victim rather than a villain. However, soldiers cannot be indifferent to the fact that, in conflict after conflict, their effort and sacrifice do not have the strategic effect that was desired and expected. It is a conclusion of this monograph that the Army, indeed each of the services, needs to think much harder about strategy than it has in the past. There is a sense in which strategy, naturally, is above the pay grade of nearly everyone in the military. This condition was greatly accentuated by the Goldwater-Nichols Act (1986) and the way in which the act was implemented. The Army cannot be indifferent to the strategic consequences of its military behavior. Not least must this be true because, in its drive for transformation, it is striving to be adaptable to a new context populated by asymmetric enemies and protracted conflicts. Once the Army grants that its tactical and operational actions have strategic meaning, which in its turn has to have political meaning, it can track back and reconsider whether its tactical habits and preferences may benefit from some further adaptation to circumstances. Soldiers have to clear their mind of the belief that they do not "do strategy." If they will read Chapter 33 of Lawrence's *Seven Pillars of Wisdom*, they will discover, or be reminded of, "the false antithesis between strategy . . . and tactics." Lawrence concluded that strategy and tactics "seemed only points of view from which to ponder the elements of war. . . ."[93] Leaders of the armed forces, senior officials in the national security bureaucracy, and assorted experts and would-be opinion leaders talk perennially about strategy. And yet, somehow, often in practice American strategic performance bears a close resemblance to the view of strategy expressed by Field Marshal Helmuth Graf von Moltke, the Prussian victor in two of the Wars of German Unification (1866, 1870-71). Having explained the nature of strategy in sound Clausewitzian terms, the Field Marshal proceeded to turn the master's theory on its head. He advised that "[t]he demands of strategy grow silent in the face of a tactical victory and adapt themselves to the newly created situation. *Strategy is a system of expedients.*"[94] The events of 1914-18 and 1939-45 bear eloquent witness to the consequences of Moltke's logic. To direct attention to America's strategy deficit is not to make a fine academic point, the kind of claim to be expected of a theorist. This deficiency lies at the heart of the country's difficulties in its protracted struggles with irregular enemies. After all, American strategy is about the threat or use of force for its political ends. If

America performs poorly at the strategic level, much of the cost and effort of the Army's transformation will be wasted on efforts ill suited to the political tasks prescribed by policy.

The third conclusion of the monograph is that there is a traditional American way of war which, in some respects, encourages a military style that is far from optimal as an approach to the challenges posed by irregular enemies. I do not wish to be misunderstood. I am not quite arguing that the American way of war, a style reflecting cultural influences, will thwart the ambitions for transformation, though there are grounds for anxiety in this regard. Also, I am certainly not claiming that a way of war is immutable. A way does evolve and may adapt, but it does so slowly. After all, it is deeply rooted in history, and there are good reasons why it is what it is. Also, let me emphasize, although I am concerned to point up its weaknesses, especially its strategic deficiencies, the American way of war has major characteristic strengths. Indeed, if it did not have such strengths, it would not have been adopted, and it would not have persisted. Not everyone will agree with each characteristic I have discerned in the American way; there is no authorized list. But this analysis rests on the strong conviction that there has been and is such a "way," and that its strength will be a problem, perhaps a severe problem, for the process of transformation and adaptation. Especially is the American way of war likely to be a problem, really a harassing condition, for a transformation that focuses significantly on the ability to conduct warfare against irregular enemies. In these concluding paragraphs, it is probably useful to provide a terse reminder of the leading characteristics of "the American way."

1. Apolitical	8. Large-scale
2. Astrategic	9. Aggressive, offensive
3. Ahistorical	10. Profoundly regular
4. Problem-solving, optimistic	11. Impatient
5. Culturally challenged	12. Logistically excellent
6. Technology dependent	13. Highly sensitive to casualties
7. Focused on firepower	

Characteristics of "the American Way."

Previously we have shown how inappropriate many features of the traditional American way of war tend to be for a struggle against irregular enemies. The dependence on technology, the reliance on firepower, the emphasis on U.S. casualty avoidance, for leading examples, express a mindset and doctrine that have not adapted persuasively to the distinctive conditions of irregular warfare. As the leading power willing and able to undertake tasks on behalf of global order and stability, however, the United States dare not assume that all its future foes will be of an irregular character. This means that the armed forces, and the Army in particular, cannot "lighten up" comprehensively in order to meet the challenges posed by terrorists and insurgents. Assuredly, there will be regular enemies in America's strategic future, even if they are obliged by America's strengths to fight in irregular ways. We have to beware of drawing a misleadingly neat distinction between regular and irregular enemies and modes of struggle.

The Army has stated clearly enough in official documents that it is aware of some of the problems addressed in this monograph. Indeed, the Army's transformation strategy is proclaimed to have "three components: transformed culture; transformed processes; transformed capabilities."[95] The intent is praiseworthy and sound. But does the Army of today appreciate the full scope and depth of the way of war that it has inherited? This monograph has been designed not so much to attempt to bring new facts about irregular warfare to the attention of soldiers. I assume that the problem of irregular and asymmetric foes is well enough understood already. Rather, my purpose is to show the scope and depth of the challenge of cultural change. It will be no small accomplishment to effect radical change in a traditional way of war. Especially will this be so when the effectiveness of that "way" will be enhanced by the prodigious high-technology innovations to which the Department of Defense is committed with its vision of transformation. Self-knowledge is vital. This monograph invites American soldiers to look at their own public, strategic, and military culture, and then consider how much change is needed if they are to be competitive with irregular enemies.

The three major elements in my argument—irregular enemies, strategy, and the traditional American way of war—come together in my third conclusion. U.S. strategic effectiveness will not be challenged successfully by truly more competent enemies, but it may fall short for reasons of America's own political, strategic, and military culture. As we have argued before, the problems are twofold. Americans need not only to understand that irregular warfare is different tactically and operationally from a regular struggle; scarcely less important, Americans must never forget that strategy must rule all of warfare, regular and irregular. The traditional American way of war was designed to take down regular enemies, and was not overly attentive to the strategic effect and political consequences of military action. That legacy makes the task before the agents of transformation and adaptation even greater than perhaps they have realized to date. This monograph should be helpful in assisting understanding of the structure of the challenge faced by the Army today.

The subtitle of this monograph poses the question, "Can the American Way of War Adapt?" My answer is "perhaps, but only with difficulty." Cultural change cannot reliably be implemented by plans, orders, and exhortation. Even negative experience is not entirely to be trusted as a certain source of sound education (remember Vietnam!). What we do know is that the prospects for effecting the transformation necessary to meet irregular enemies must be much improved if the scope and scale of the challenge are recognized honestly.

ENDNOTES

1. Stuart Kinross, "Clausewitz and Low-Intensity Conflict," *The Journal of Strategic Studies*, Vol. 27, No. 1, March 2004, p. 54.

2. Sam C. Sarkesian, *America's Forgotten Wars: The Counterrevolutionary Past and Lessons for the Future*, Westport, CT: Greenwood Press, 1984, p. 245.

3. Charles E. Callwell, *Small Wars: A Tactical Textbook for Imperial Soldiers*, London: Greenhill Books, 1990 (first published 1906), p. 23.

4. The cyclical view of strategic history is presented and defended in Colin S. Gray, *Another Bloody Century: Future Warfare*, London: Weidenfeld and Nicolson, 2005.

5. Carl von Clausewitz, *On War*, Michael Howard and Peter Paret, trans., Princeton, NJ: Princeton University Press, 1976, pp. 141, 578 (hereafter cited as Clausewitz).

6. Colin S. Gray, *Villains, Victims and Sheriffs: Strategic Studies for an Inter-War Period,* An inaugural lecture at the University of Hull, January 12, 1994, Hull, UK: University of Hull Press, 1994. Reprinted in *Comparative Strategy*, Vol. 13, No. 4, October-December 1994, pp. 353-369.

7. Donald H. Rumsfeld, *The National Defense Strategy of the United States of America*, Washington, DC: U.S. Department of Defense, March 2005, p. 1.

8. See Colin S. Gray, *The Sheriff: America's Defense of the New World Order*, Lexington, KY: University Press of Kentucky, 2004. I seem to specialize in controversial concepts and metaphors. My characterization of the United States as the contemporary global sheriff is about as popular as was my description of the 1990s as an interwar period.

9. Raymond Aron, "The Evolution of Modern Strategic Thought," in Alastair Buchan, ed., *Problems of Modern Strategy*, London: ISS, 1970, p. 25.

10. Callwell, *Small Wars*, p. 21.

11. Thomas X. Hammes, *The Sling and the Stone: On War in the 21st Century*, St. Paul, MN: Zenith Press, 2004.

12. For some basic education, see Clausewitz, esp. Book 3, ch. 1. Also see Colin S. Gray, *Modern Strategy*, Oxford: Oxford University Press, 1999, ch. 1; Richard K. Betts, "Is Strategy an Illusion?" *International Security*, Vol. 25, No. 2, Fall 2000, pp. 5-50; and Hew Strachan, "The Lost Meaning of Strategy," *Survival*, Vol. 47, No. 3, Autumn 2005, pp. 33-54.

13. Sun-tzu, *The Art of War*, Ralph D. Sawyer, trans., Boulder, CO: Westview Press, 1994; Robert B. Strassler, ed., *The Landmark Thucydides: A Comprehensive Guide to "The Peloponnesian War,"* Richard Crawley, trans., rev. edn., New York: Free Press, 1996.

14. I was tempted to claim that intellectual mastery of the strategic mode of reasoning equips one to succeed in war, regular or irregular. Indeed, I included that claim in the keynote speech which was the basis of this monograph. On further reflection, however, it rapidly became clear that, although skill as a strategist is always desirable, it cannot guarantee decisive victory. The enemy may be led by strategists who are yet more skilled strategically, or, more likely, the balance of advantages and disadvantages may be so heavily weighted to one side or the other that no measure of strategic excellence is able to provide sufficient compensation. In the text, I warn against treating COIN theory and the discovery of culture as panaceas. I could just as well warn against the elevation of strategy to panacea status. The American defense community periodically, albeit briefly, succumbs to what can fairly be termed "strategism," meaning an infatuation with strategy.

15. I have developed this argument in some detail in my monograph, *Transformation and Strategic Surprise*, Carlisle Barracks, PA: Strategic Studies Institute, U.S. Army War College, April 2005.

16. Andrew F. Krepinevich, Jr., *The Army and Vietnam*, Baltimore: Johns Hopkins University Press, 1986, ch. 6.

17. Clausewitz, p. 177.

18. Russell F. Weigley, *The American Way of War: A History of United States Strategy and Policy*, New York: Macmillan, 1973, is now the classic treatment of this contestable concept.

19. Sun-tzu, *Art of War*, p. 179.

20. In the 1970s, a few, a very few, American defense analysts and regional experts made the startling suggestion that the Soviet Union might not have bought into a common nuclear policy enlightenment. Significant period pieces included: Richard Pipes, "Why the Soviet Union Thinks It could Fight and Win a Nuclear War," *Commentary*, Vol. 64, No. 1, July 1977, pp. 21-34; Jack L. Snyder, *The Soviet Strategic Culture: Implications for Limited Nuclear Operations*, R-2154-AF, Santa Monica, CA: RAND, September 1977; and Fritz Ermath, "Contrasts in American and Soviet Strategic Thought," *International Security*, Vol. 3, No. 2, Fall 1978, pp. 138-155.

21. Robert H. Scales, Jr., "Culture-Centric Warfare," *U.S. Naval Institute Proceedings*, Vol. 130, No. 10, October 2004, pp. 32-36.

22. The clearest statement of this fact is in Samuel P. Huntington, *American Military Strategy*, Policy Paper 28, Berkeley, CA: Institute of International Studies, University of California, Berkeley, 1986.

23. Mao Tse-tung, *Selected Military Writings*, Beijing: Foreign Languages Press, 1963.

24. Robert R. Tomes, "Relearning Counterinsurgency Warfare," *Parameters*, Vol. XXXIV, No. 1, Spring 2004, pp. 16-28, is very much to the point. From a very large literature, Ian F. W. Beckett, *Modern Insurgencies and Counter-Insurgencies: Guerrillas and their Opponents since 1750*, London: Routledge, 2001, provides invaluable historical perspective, while Donald W. Hamilton, *The Art of Insurgency: American Military Policy and the Failure of Strategy in Southeast Asia*, Westport, CT: Praeger Publishers, 1998, is a usefully focused study.

25. Later on in the text I explain the principal characteristics of COIN. I do this not because I believe that the U.S. Army does not understand them. Rather is the intention both to provide a reminder of "the basics" and, more particularly, to showcase the contrast between irregular warfare and America's preferred regular style. With regard to my working assumption that the historically attested principles of COIN are well and widely appreciated, some readers of this monograph may be of the opinion that it is not as well-founded as I would like to believe.

26. Steven Metz and Raymond Millen, *Insurgency and Counterinsurgency in the 21st Century: Reconceptualizing Threat and Response*, Carlisle Barracks, PA: U.S. Army War College, Strategic Studies Institute, November 2004; Michael F. Morris, "Al Qaeda as Insurgency," *Joint Force Quarterly*, No. 39, 4th Qtr. 2005, pp. 41-50.

27. Ralph Peters, "In Praise of Attrition," *Parameters*, Vol. XXXIV, No. 2, Summer 2004, pp. 24-32.

28. The use of time as a weapon to outlast the regular *foreign* enemy of an insurgency is a significant theme in Jeffrey Record, *The Wrong War: Why We Lost in Vietnam*, Annapolis, MD: Naval Institute Press, 1998, e.g., pp. 67, 178-179.

29. See Susan L. Marquis, *Unconventional Warfare: Rebuilding U.S. Special Operations Forces*, Washington, DC: Brookings Institution Press, 1997.

30. I develop this argument in "From Principles of Warfare to Principles of War: A Clausewitzian Solution," in *Transformation and Strategic Surprise;* and *Strategy and History: Essays on Theory and Practice*, London: Routledge, 2006, pp. 81-87.

31. Clausewitz, p. 178.

32. My early efforts to apply cultural analysis to contemporary strategy were focused on superpower nuclear issues. Those efforts eventually were collected in *Nuclear Strategy and National Style*, Lanham, MD: Hamilton Press, 1986. For a vigorous methodological assault on my endeavors, see Alastair Iain Johnston, *Cultural Realism: Strategic Culture and Grand Strategy in Chinese History*, Princeton, NJ: Princeton University Press, 1995, esp. ch. 1. I replied to his critique in my *Modern Strategy*, ch. 5. The primary issue between us was whether culture merely influenced behavior, or was evidenced in behavior. Johnston was seeking a methodology for the study of culture, whereas I was proceeding empirically, without overmuch concern for the feasibility of theory-building. I have always been attracted to Callwell's advice that "[t]heory cannot be accepted as conclusive when practice points the other way." *Small Wars*, p. 270. For those who wish to explore the highways and byways of strategic culture, they could do worse than sample the following: Ken Booth, *Strategy and Ethnocentrism*, London: Croom Helm, 1979; Carl G. Jacobsen, ed., *Strategic Power: USA/USSR*, New York: St. Martin's Press, 1990; Peter J. Katzenstein, ed., *The Culture of National Security: Norms and Identity in World Politics*, New York: Columbia University Press, 1996; Michael C. Desch, "Culture Clash: Assessing the Importance of Ideas in Security Studies," *International Security*, Vol. 23, No. 1, Summer 1998, pp. 141-170; Victor Davis Hanson, *Why the West Has Won: Carnage and Culture from Salamis to Vietnam*, London: Faber and Faber, 2001; and for a more critical view of culture's strategic responsibility, see John A. Lynn, *Battle: A History of Combat and Culture: From Ancient Greece to Modern America*, Boulder, CO: Westview Press, 2003; John Glenn, Darryl Howlett, and Stuart Poore, eds., *Neorealism Versus Strategic Culture*, Aldershot, UK: Ashgate, 2004; and the sources I cite in *Transformation and Strategic Surprise*, n. 46.

33. Eliot A. Cohen, *Supreme Command: Soldiers, Statesmen, and Leadership in Wartime*, New York: Free Press, 2002, is essential contemporary reading on American civil-military relations. The "normal" American theory of those relations, which describes and praises the separation of soldiers from politics, was presented in the classic study by Samuel P. Huntington, *The Soldier and the State: The Theory and Politics of Civil-Military Relations*, Cambridge, MA: Harvard University Press, 1957.

34. Clausewitz, pp. 177 ff.

35. Cohen, *Supreme Command*.

36. Clausewitz, pp. 610, 607.

37. *Ibid.*, p. 605.

38. The contemporary literature addressing the difficulties of strategic performance directly is not extensive, but most people should find it highly useful. For some examples, see David Jablonsky, "Why Is Strategy Difficult?" in Gary L. Guertner, ed., *The Search for Strategy: Politics and Strategic Vision*, Westport, CT: Greenwood Press, 1993, pp. 3-45; Colin S. Gray, "Why Strategy Is Difficult," *Joint Force Quarterly*, No. 22, Summer 1999, pp. 6-12; and Richard K. Betts, "The Trouble with Strategy: Bridging Policy and Operations," *Joint Force Quarterly*, No. 29, Autumn/Winter 2001-02, pp. 23-30.

39. Clausewitz, p. 101.

40. *Ibid.*, p. 608.

41. Cohen's brilliant *Supreme Command* is essential, but by no means is it the last word on the subject.

42. This theorist feels a little uncomfortable quoting this ironic cliché. At a recent AWC/SSI conference, he was told by the former soldier who was the source of the deadly admission, that he misspoke in stressful circumstances and could not clarify his meaning or retract the phrase before the damage was done. Friction happens! I hope that the person in question can find it in his generous heart to forgive me.

43. Clausewitz, p. 104.

44. *Ibid.*, pp. 88-89.

45. Especially useful studies include J. Paul de B. Taillon, *The Evolution of Special Forces in Counter-Terrorism: The British and American Experience*, Westport, CT: Praeger Publishers, 2001; Alastair Finlan, "Warfare by Other Means: Special Forces, Terrorism and Grand Strategy," in Thomas R. Mockaitis and Paul B. Rich, eds., *Grand Strategy in the War Against Terrorism*, London: Frank Cass, 2003, pp. 92-108; and, preeminently, James D. Kiras, *Rendering the Mortal Blow Easier: Special Operations and the Nature of Strategy*, London: Routledge, forthcoming 2006.

46. Three first-rate books by Lewis Sorley are essential reading: *Thunderbolt: From the Battle of the Bulge to Vietnam and Beyond: General Creighton Abrams and the Army of His Times*, New York: Simon and Schuster, 1997; particularly his *A Better War: The Unexamined Victories and Final Tragedy of America's Last Years in Vietnam*, New York: Harcourt Brace, 1999; and *Honorable Warrior: General Harold K. Johnson and the Ethics of Command*, Lawrence, KS: University Press of Kansas, 1998. My monograph is not specifically about Vietnam, but that war keeps intruding into the narrative and analysis despite my best efforts to minimize the intrusion. Most of the literature, and certainly the overwhelming bulk of expert opinion on America's performance—political, strategic, and military—is, on balance, strongly negative. Therefore, for some balance, it is suitable to recommend two thoughtful books,

one based on firsthand (Australian) experience, which tell a rather more up-beat story of the American effort in Vietnam: Mark W. Woodruff, *Unheralded Victory: Who Won the Vietnam War?* New York: HarperCollins, 1999; and C. Dale Walton, *The Myth of Inevitable U.S. Defeat in Vietnam*, London: Frank Cass, 2002. There is no question that Americans can be effective in the conduct of irregular warfare against revolutionary enemies. For example, see Michael A. Hennessy, *Strategy in Vietnam: The Marines and Revolutionary Warfare in I Corps, 1965-1972*, Westport, CT: Praeger Publishers, 1997. The trouble was that the Army, by and large, was not committed to implement an effective strategy. For a longer historical perspective, Max Boot, *The Savage Wars of Peace: Small Wars and the Rise of American Power*, New York: Basic Books, 2002, is very useful.

47. Deliberately, this monograph does not delve into the controversial policy and strategy realm of "the Bush Doctrine," which licenses the option of taking preventive or preemptive cross-border action against enemies of any kind, states, or organized groups or movements. Plainly, the kind of bold, hopefully rapidly decisive military action required for such attacks is all but designed for its close fit with the traditional American way of war, though a few nontrivial caveats need noting. U.S. intelligence, though generally excellent technically, has been anything but excellent in its human dimension, on the targets at issue, or in the assessments reached in Washington. Also, America's habit of separating war and policy, thereby helping to produce an acute strategy deficit, renders surprise attacks on foreign soil an exceptionally hazardous option for the American upholder of global law and order. At present, I am working on a study to examine this issue in a detailed and systematic way. At present, the strategic studies literature offers almost nothing of solid value on preemption and prevention as policy choices and consequent strategies. What we do have available by and large are leftovers from the strategic thought and doctrine of the Cold War, where we briefly debated preventive war, and much more seriously considered launch-on-warning and launch-under-attack for our strategic nuclear forces.

48. Some worrying possibilities are discussed in the influential article, "Command of the Commons: The Military Foundation of U.S. Hegemony," *International Security*, Vol. 28, No. 1, Summer 2003, pp. 5-46. Posen is not enthusiastic about American commitments to continental warfare.

49. Krepinevich, *The Army and Vietnam*, p. 7 (emphasis in the original).

50. For my extensive discussion of this subject, see *Another Bloody Century*, ch. 6, "Irregular Warfare and Terrorism."

51. Clausewitz's chapter on "The People in Arms" recognized the occasional potency of guerrilla action, in particular as a military tactic by an outraged people against an invader. Such warfare was extensive in the years that he had lived through as a serving soldier. But, sensibly enough, he recognized that the irregulars could succeed only in highly permissive circumstances. Clausewitz, Book 6, ch. 26. Certainly it is true to claim that he devoted very little explicit attention to people's war in its several styles. Nonetheless, I believe that Ian Beckett's fairly unappreciative comments on Clausewitz's treatment of guerrilla warfare are too

negative. *Modern Insurgencies and Counter-Insurgencies*, p. 14. In fact, Clausewitz theorized even better than he may have known for irregular warfare, as this monograph argues. Also, see Kinross, "Clausewitz and Low-Intensity Conflict."

52. See Roger Trinquier, *Modern Warfare: A French View of Counterinsurgency*, New York: Praeger, 1964; and for a judicious explanation, Peter Paret, *French Revolutionary Warfare from Indo-China to Algeria: The Analysis of a Political and Military Doctrine*, New York: Frederick A. Praeger, 1964.

53. Callwell, *Small Wars*, p. 38.

54. Clausewitz, p. 605.

55. For a persuasive set of scholarly studies of the phenomenon of cultural adaptation, see Emily O. Goldman and Leslie C. Eliason, eds., *The Diffusion of Military Technology and Ideas*, Stanford, CA: Stanford University Press, 2003. Williamson Murray and Allan R. Millett, eds., *Military Innovation in the Interwar Period*, Cambridge: Cambridge University Press, 1996, also have much of value to say on the subject of distinctive national responses to common new technological opportunities.

56. "Soft power" is shorthand for the many means of gaining influence available in principle to American grand strategists short of threatening or taking action that must kill people and break things. The founding modern text is Joseph S. Nye, Jr., *Bound to Lead: The Changing Nature of American Power*, New York: Basic Books, 1990. Naturally, it is an attractive concept. It is a little less attractive in conflicts with rogues and irregulars because they tend to be less easily seduced by some aspect of American culture and ideology than are more normal aspirants for the better, which is to say American, way of life. Also, the appealing belief that the slow but cumulatively engaging potency of our soft power should preclude the necessity for our having to resort to brutal hard power, may simply be wrong. The trouble is that when soft power fails over a lengthy period, time, that most unforgiving dimension of strategy, will have been lost for truly effective action. The case of Iran today promises to be a classic case in illustration of this point, alas.

57. T. E. Lawrence, "Guerrilla Warfare," entry in *Encyclopedia Britannica: A New Survey of Universal Knowledge*, Vol. 10, London: Encyclopedia Britannica, 14th edn. 1929, 1959 revision, esp. p. 950B. In his *Seven Pillars of Wisdom: A Triumph*, New York: Doubleday, 1991 edn., Lawrence drew upon the insight that "[i]t seemed a regular soldier might be helpless without a target, owning only what he sat on, and subjugating only what, by order, he could poke his rifle at" (p. 192). His undoubted brilliance as a practitioner and theorist of guerrilla warfare is not well-communicated, even to this admirer, by his purple prose, overstatements, underappreciation of the salience of context, and vanity. Still, the high quality of his thought and his record of success do survive his literary pretensions.

58. This important but frequently overlooked point is made most usefully in Adam Roberts, "The 'War on Terror' in Historical Perspective," *Survival*, Vol. 47, No. 2, Summer 2005, p. 112.

59. An essay in my *History and Strategy* book compares and contrasts the two concepts of Principles of Warfare and Principles of War, and suggests candidates for the latter list.

60. See Gray, *Transformation and Strategic Surprise*.

61. See Stephen Peter Rosen, "Vietnam and the American Theory of Limited War," *International Security*, Vol. 7, No. 2, Fall 1982, pp. 83-113; Mark Clodfelter, *The Limits of Air Power: The American Bombing of North Vietnam*, New York: Free Press, 1989; and Robert A. Pape, *Bombing to Win: Air Power and Coercion in War*, Ithaca, NY: Cornell University Press, 1996, ch. 6.

62. Clausewitz, *On War*, p. 605. The intellectual godfather of coercive diplomacy, American-style, was Thomas C. Schelling. See his timely and influential tour de force, *Arms and Influence*, New Haven, CT: Yale University Press, 1966. Another very American period piece which had real-world consequence was Herman Kahn, *On Escalation: Metaphors and Scenarios*, New York: Praeger, 1965.

63. Huntington, *American Military Strategy*, p. 16.

64. Geoffrey Till, *Maritime Strategy and the Nuclear Age*, London: Macmillan, 1982, pp. 224-225.

65. Sarkesian, *America's Forgotten Wars*; John M. Collins, *America's Small Wars: Lessons for the Future*, Washington, DC: Brassey's (U.S.), 1991; and Boot, *The Savage Wars of Peace*.

66. Bernard Brodie, "The Continuing Relevance of *On War*," in Clausewitz, p. 54.

67. See Stanley Hoffman, *Gulliver's Troubles: On the Setting of American Foreign Policy*, New York: McGraw-Hill, 1968.

68. Scales, "Culture-Centric Warfare."

69. Eliot A. Cohen: "The Mystique of U.S. Air Power," *Foreign Affairs*, Vol. 73, No. 1, January/February 1994, pp. 109-124; and "The Meaning and Future of Air Power," *Orbis*, Vol. 39, No. 2, Spring 1995, pp. 189-200. In addition, for careful historical perspective, Benjamin S. Lambeth, *The Transformation of American Air Power*, Ithaca, NY: Cornell University Press, 2000, is essential.

70. See, e.g., U.S. Army, *2004 Army Transformation Roadmap*, Washington, DC: Office of the Deputy Chief of Staff, U.S. Army Operations, Army Transformation Office, July 2004.

71. Two British COIN experts judge that "[g]enerally speaking the less sophisticated the army, the better able it has been to defeat insurgency." F. W. Beckett and John Pimlott, "Introduction," to Beckett and Pimlott, eds., *Armed Forces and Modern Counter-Insurgency*, New York: St. Martin's Press, 1985, p. 10. A similarly reserved attitude towards technology has been expressed recently by the outstanding British soldier of his generation, a man with an abundance of relevant personal experience: General Sir Rupert Smith, *The Utility of Force: The Art of War in the Modern World*, London: Allen Lane, 2005, esp., pp. 400-401. Many

of his comments echo the standard empirically-based lore on how to wage COIN intelligently. It is worth noting that probably the dominant concept in Smith's book is his belief that today, and in the future, the chief challenge facing Western armies will be the necessity to function effectively "amongst the people."

72. Quoted in Boot, *The Savage Wars of Peace*, p. 294.

73. The bluntest competent assault to date on this military cultural preference is to be found in Frederick W. Kagan, "War and Aftermath," *Policy Review*, No. 120, August and September 2003, p. 27. "It is a fundamental mistake to see the enemy as a set of targets. The enemy in war is a group of people."

74. Boot, *The Savage Wars of Peace*, p. 301. In 1966, for example, two-thirds of the American shells expended were fired at no known targets. Also see Record, *The Wrong War*, ch. 3.

75. Huntington, *American Military Strategy*, p. 15.

76. *Ibid.*, p. 16.

77. The pattern of military sacrifice mandated by a public culture of unpreparedness is well told in Charles E. Heller and William A. Stofft, eds., *America's First Battles, 1776-1965*, Lawrence, KS: University Press of Kansas, 1986; see esp. ch. 9 on Korea.

78. This is not to deny that small SOF training teams can make, indeed have and should be allowed to make, a crucial difference in the ability of local clients to combat insurgents and terrorists. However, there are no free gifts in warfare. Even a well-conducted advisory enterprise carries the risk of donating to the irregular enemy visible evidence both of American imperialism and of official dependency upon the hated outsider.

79. See Sarkesian, *America's Forgotten Wars*; Collins, *America's Small Wars*; Anthony James Joes, *America and Guerrilla Warfare*, Lexington, KY: University Press of Kentucky, 2000; and Boot, *The Savage Wars of Peace*.

80. See Krepinevich, *The Army and Vietnam*.

81. For an important study from the period, a true period piece, written by a gifted and highly experienced British serving soldier, see Frank Kitson, *Low Intensity Operations*, London: Faber and Faber, 1971.

82. Krepinevich, *The Army and Vietnam*, pp. 230-232.

83. I explored the conditions permissive for the success of SO in my "Handfuls of Heroes on Desperate Ventures: When do Special Operations Succeed?" *Parameters*, Vol. XXIX, No. 2, Spring 1999, pp. 2-24. I suspect strongly that by emphasizing SO as unconventional warfare, I may well have appeared to undervalue SOF in their several COIN roles.

84. Mao Tse-tung, "On Protracted War (May 1938)," in *Selected Military Writings*, pp. 187-266.

85. See Herman Hattaway and Archer Jones, *How the North Won: A Military History of the Civil War*, Urbana, IL: University of Illinois Press, 1983, p. 720, for

the primacy of logistics; and Thomas M. Kane, *Military Logistics and Strategic Performance*, London: Frank Cass, 2001, for a superior explanation of logistics as an essential enabler of strategy

86. Henry E. Eccles, *Military Concepts and Philosophy*, New Brunswick, NJ: Rutgers University Press, 1965, p. 83. "[A]ll logistic activities naturally tend to grow to inordinate size, and unless positive control is maintained, this growth continues until, like a ball of wet snow, a huge accumulation of slush obscures the hard core of essential combat support, and the mass becomes unmanageable. This snowball effect permeates the entire structure of military organization and effort."

87. Alfred Thayer Mahan, *The Influence of Sea Power upon History, 1660-1783*, London: Methuen,1965, p. 25; Barry R. Posen, "Command of the Commons."

88. Peter M. Dunn, "The American Army: The Vietnam War, 1965-1973," in Beckett and Pimlott, eds., *Armed Forces and Modern Counter-Insurgency*, p. 103.

89. Peter D. Feaver and Richard H. Kohn, eds., *Soldiers and Civilians: The Civil-Military Gap and American National Security*, Cambridge, MA: MIT Press, 2001. Also see Paul Cornish, "Myth and Reality: U.S. and U.K. Approaches to Casualty Aversion and Force Protection," *Defense Studies*, Vol. 3, No. 2, Summer 2003, pp. 121-128.

90. Callwell, *Small Wars*, p. 90.

91. That development is well-handled in Beckett, *Modern Insurgencies and Counter-Insurgencies*.

92. Mary Kaldor, "Elaborating the 'New War' Thesis," in Isabelle Duyvesteyn and Jan Angstrom, eds., *Rethinking the Nature of War*, London: Frank Cass, 2005, pp. 210-224; Hammes, *The Sling and the Stone*.

93. Lawrence, *Seven Pillars of Wisdom*, p. 192.

94. Daniel J. Hughes, ed., *Moltke on the Art of War: Selected Writings*, Novato, CA: Presidio Press, 1993, p. 47 (emphasis added).

95. U.S. Army, *2004 Transformation Roadmap*, p. viii.